Business Arabic

Business Arabic

A Comprehensive Vocabulary

Second Edition

Mai Zaki & John Mace

Georgetown University Press /
Washington, DC

First published in the United Kingdom by
Edinburgh University Press.

ISBN 978-1-64712-161-7 (paperback)
ISBN 978-1-64712-162-4 (ebook)

Library of Congress Control Number: 2021932622

22 21   9 8 7 6 5 4 3 2 First printing

CONTENTS

INTRODUCTION

Like the first edition of this book, this second edition aims to help students of Arabic, whether at university or in the workplace, to handle confidently Arabic business vocabulary. It can be used either as support for a business-oriented Arabic course, or for translation studies, or as an extension of general Arabic studies. In this edition the earlier material has been thoroughly edited and revised, and 743 new entries have been added to cover developments in business, including terms related to globalisation and innovation in modern business. American and British terms and spelling are both shown.

The entries are listed in Arabic alphabetical order within each of the ten chapters, the article الـ... and all prepositions being disregarded. The English equivalents of all entries are repeated in the Index, enabling reference or translation into Arabic.

Chapter 1 lists terms of general use (including generally applicable names of international institutions) and specialised terms for which there is no chapter in the book. Wherever appropriate, specialised terms are listed for preference in Chapters 2 to 10. The same term may appear with different meanings or uses in different chapters.

Pointing in this vocabulary

The pointing is selective, i.e. marked only where the pronunciation is not clear from spelling or grammar:

- *hamzat al-qat'* is always shown.
- *shadda* is always shown, except on the masculine *nisba* ending ي.

- The one-letter words ب, ل and و are pointed only when prefixed.
- Unless spelling, pointing or grammar indicate otherwise, read the weak letters so: medial ا as long *ā,* و as long *ū,* ي as long *ī;* and hamzated forms أ as short *'a/a',* ؤ as short *'u/u'* and ﺌ/ئ as short *'i/i'.*
- Final ي (dotted) is always the letter *yā',* and ى (undotted) always *'alif maqṣūra.*
- A single *fatḥa* before ة and ى is in general not marked.
- Cross-references are unpointed except for *shadda, hamzat al-qaṭ',* and *tanwīn* (for the last of which see *Inflection* below).

Nouns, adjectives and adverbs are shown as follows:
- *Gender:* only where not clear from the spelling or meaning.
- *Isolated adjectives:* masculine singular, unless stated otherwise.
- *Inflection:* only *tanwīn* in weak, predicative, or adverbial forms.
- *Plural:* after the singular form, but only where broken or irregular, introduced by the Arabic abbreviation ج. A sound plural as alternative is marked 'sound\' after the broken plural. The sign → refers a broken or irregular plural to the entry in singular form, except where both entries would be adjacent. In compound expressions the plural is not added.

Verbs are shown as follows:
- *Form I triliteral:* first principal part (i.e. past or perfect tense, هو form) with pointing of vowels other than the personal ending; the government if this differs from the English; the verbal noun (مصدر); the notation I; and the variable second vowel (shown

as *a/u/i*) of the second principal part (i.e. present or imperfect tense, هو form).

- *Forms II-X triliteral:* first principal part; the government if this differs from the English; and the notation II to X.
- *Form I quadriliteral:* as for Form II triliteral, but with notation IQ and the verbal noun.
- *Participle, Verbal Noun:* listed as a separate entry in cases of special meaning, special or frequent use, or difficulty.
- *Prepositional object:* The preposition is shown, with the animate object and inanimate object in that order where both apply.

Abbreviations and symbols used in the vocabulary indicate:

adj.	adjective	Q	quadriliteral
adv.	adverb	s.	singular
cst.	construct (إضافة)	s.o.	someone
e.o.	each other	s.t.	something
f.	feminine	vb.	verb(al)
I-X	verb form	ج	broken/irregular plural
intr.	intransitive	ه	animate direct object
m.	masculine	ﻪ	inanimate direct object
n.	noun	\, /	or
pl.	plural	( )	optional

Our thanks go to Kifah Hanna for her valuable revision and improvement of the draft text of the previous edition before its publication. For this present edition Marilyn Moore gave patient and painstaking help with the English Index. Any remaining errors or shortcomings in the text are our own responsibility.

1. GENERAL

اِبْتِداءً من	with effect from
اِبْتِدائي	initial, preliminary
اِتِّجاه	trend
اِتِّحاد	union
الاتِّحاد الأُوروبّي	European Union
اِتِّخاذ القَرارات	decision-taking (n.)
اِتِّفاقيّة	agreement
الاتِّفاقيّة العامّة لِلتَعْريفات	General Agreement on Tariffs
الجُمْرُكيّة وَالتِجارة (الجات)	and Trade, GATT
اتّفق مع على VIII	to agree with s.o. on s.t.
إجْراء	procedure, measure
أجّل II	to postpone, defer
أحادي الجانِب	unilateral
اِحْتِباس حَراري	global warming
احتكر VIII	to monopolise
اِحْتِكار	monopoly
اِحْتِكار القِلّة	oligopoly
اِحْتِياطي reserve (n.), see نظام	
إحصاء see علم	
إحْصائي	statistical, statistician

إحْصائيّات statistics

اِخْتِيار choice

أَخَذَ بِعَيْن الاِعْتِبار to take into consideration

خطأ → أخطاء

خلق → أخلاق

أخير see موعد

أدار ه IV to manage, direct

إدارة management, administration,

see مجلس

إدارة بِالأَهْداف management by objectives

الأَدْنى minimum

أرجأ IV to postpone, defer

رقم → أرقام

ازداد VIII to increase intr.

اِزْدِهار prosperity

أزْمة ج أزَمات crisis

أساس ج أُسُس basis \sound

دراسة , أسلوب see → أساليب

سبب → أسباب

اِسْتِهْلاكيّة consumerism

اِسْتِدامة sustainability

اِسْتْراتيجيّة strategy

استشار X to consult

اِسْتِشاري advisory

اِسْتِقْرار stability

استهلك X to consume

أسّس II to establish, found, incorporate

أساس ← أسس

أُسْلوب ج أساليب method, system, technique

اشترك VIII to participate, cooperate

أشرف على IV to supervise

الشّرِكة الأُمّ parent company

شغل ← أشغال

أشْغال (عُموميّة\مَدَنيّة) (public/civil) works

متعدّد , ثلاثي see أطراف

اِعْتِبار consideration, opinion, regard,

see أخذ

اِعْتِبارًا ل in view of

اِعْتِبارًا من with effect from

اعتبر VIII to consider

عضو ← أعضاء

أعلن عن مُناقَصة IV to call for tenders

أعْمال business, ← عمل , see أمّ, رجل pl.

أغْلَبيّة majority

افتتح VIII to inaugurate

إقليم ← أقاليم

اِقْتِصاد جُزئي microeconomics

اِقْتِصاد حُرّ laissez-faire economy

اِقْتِصاد سوق market economy

اِقْتِصاد كُلّي macroeconomics

اِقْتِصاد مُتَقَدِّم developed economy

اِقْتِصاد نامٍ developing economy

قسم ← أقسام

الأقْصى maximum

إقْليم ج أقاليم region

أقَلِّيّة minority

أكْثَريّة majority

أكّد II to confirm, substantiate

أكيد certain, sure (of things)

ألغى IV to cancel

مكان ← أماكن

أُمّ see شركة

أُمّ وَسَيِّدة أعْمال mumpreneur

أمْر ج أمور affair, matter

مكان ← أمكنة

أمّم II to nationalise

أَمْن security

أمر → أُمور

أمين عامّ secretary-general

اِنْتِعاش boom

انتهز فُرْصة VIII to seize an opportunity

اندماج merger

أَنْجَز IV to implement

انحرف (عن) VII to deviate (from)

انخفض intr. VII to decrease, be reduced

أنشأ IV to establish

أنشطة see شركة

نظام → أنظمة

إنْفاق عامّ public spending

اِنْفِرادي unilateral

انهار VII to collapse, crash

هدف ,see إدارة → أهداف

أوبيك see منظّمة

أوروبّي see اتّحاد

أوْلَوِيّة priority

إيجابي positive

بَحَث ه\عن بَحْث ج بُحوث I a to search for, to look into

بَرْنامَج ج بَرامِج program(me)

بِضاعة ج بَضائع ware, goods, merchandise

بَقِيّة ج بَقايا remainder

بَلَغ ه بُلوغ I u to amount to

البَنْك الدُوَلي World Bank

بيروقْراطيّة bureaucracy

بيئة environment

تابِع ج تُبّاع\اتُبَّع sound\ subsidiary (adj./n.)

بِتَأْثير رَجْعي with retroactive effect

تاجِر ج تُجّار trader, merchant, dealer

تأخّر II to be delayed

تَأْييدًا ل in support of

تابع → تُبّاع\اتُبَّع

تاجر → تجّار

تِجارة trade, see اتّفاقيّة, غرفة, منظّمة

تِجارة المَحاصيل agribusiness

تِجارة عادِلة fair trade

تِجاري trading, commercial, business (adj.),

see حاجز

تَجْريبي pilot, test (adj.)

تَحْديد حُرّيّة التَصَرُّف restrictive practice

تَحْرير liberalisation

تَحْقيق investigation

تَحْلِيل كَمّي quantitative analysis

تَحْلِيل نَوْعي qualitative analysis

تخصّص V to specialise

تَدْبِير ج تَدابِير arrangement, measure

تَدَرُّج وَظِيفي chain of command

تَدْوِيل internationalisation

تَرْكِيبة سُكّانيّة demographics

تَسَلْسُل sequence, succession

تَسْلِيع commodification

تَشْغِيل operating (n.), operation

تَصَرُّف practice, see تحديد

تَصْنِيع industrialisation

تطوّر V to develop, evolve intr.

تَعاوُنيّة cooperative (n.)

تعريف see اتّفاقيّة

تغيير see سهولة

تَغْيِير مُناخي climate change

تفاوض III to negotiate

تَفْضِيل preference

تَفْوِيض السُلْطة delegation of authority

تقرير ← تقارير

تقدّم V to progress, advance intr.

تَقْرير ج تَقارير	report
تَقْييم	evaluation
تكامُل	integration
تِكْنولوجيا	technology
تَمْهيدي	preparatory, provisional, exploratory
تَمَلُّك	acquisition
تَنْظيم	(act of) organising, organisation
التَنْظيم وَطُرُق العَمَل	organisation and methods, OM
تَنْظيمي	organisational, see هيكل, مخطّط
تَنْفيذ	implementation
تنفيذي	see مدير
تَوْجيه	orientation
توسّع intr.	V to expand
توقّع	V to expect, anticipate
ثابت	see مدّة
ثِقة (من)	trust, confidence (in)
ثُلاثي الأطْراف	trilateral, tripartite
ثُنائي	bilateral
اتفاقية	see الجات
جارٍ	ongoing
جامِعة الدُوَل العَرَبيّة	League of Arab States

جانب see أحادي

جدّد II to modernise, renew

اقتصاد partial, see جُزْئي

جَماعي group (adj.)

اتّفاقيّة see جمركي

متعدّد see جنسيّة

من جِهَتَيْن bilateral(ly)

من جِهة وَاحِدة unilateral(ly)

حافِز ج حَوافِز incentive

حافظ على III to preserve, maintain

(practice, situation)

حالي current (adj.)

حَدّ ج حُدود limit, margin

حَدّي marginal

حدّ ← حدود

اقتصاد see حرّ

احتباس see حراري

تحديد freedom, see حُرِّيّة

حُسْن النيّة good faith

حَصَل على حُصول I u to attain, achieve

حقيقة ← حقائق

حقّق II to achieve

حقَّق في II to investigate

حَقْل ج حُقول field, domain

حَقيقة ج حَقائق fact

موظف see حكومي

حَلّ ج حُلول solution (of a problem)

حَلّ ه حَلّ ج حُلول I u to solve, dissolve

حَلّ المُعْضِلات\المَشاكِل problem-solving (n.)

حلّ ← حلول

حِمايَة protection (trade)

حافز ← حوافز

حَوْكَمة governance

حوّل II to transfer

خاصّ private

خاصّيّة characteristic (n.)

خاطر ب III to risk

خبير ← خبراء

خِبْرة experience, expertise

خَبير ج خُبَراء expert

سعر see خصم

خَطَأ ج أخْطاء error

خفّض II to downsize

خُلُق ج أخْلاق ethic

خاصيّة ← خوائص

خيار option

دافِع ج دوَافِع incentive

دائرة ج دَوَائر department, directorate

دائم permanent

دبّر II to arrange, devise

دِراسة الأساليب methods study

دَرَجة grade, degree

دَعَم دَعْم I a to subsidise

دَمَج في dَمْج .intr I u to merge with

دافع ← دوافع

دائرة ← دوائر

دَوْرة cycle

دَوْري periodic

دول see جامعة , منظّمة

دُوَلي international, see بنك, صندوق

ديموغْرافيا demographics

رأْسْماليّة capitalism

ربح see هامش

رُبْع سَنَوِي quarterly (adj.)

رتّب II to arrange

رَجْعِي retroactive, retrospective, reactionary, see تأثير

رَجُل أعْمال entrepreneur

رجوع see لا

رخّص ل ب\في II to license, authorise

رُخْصة ج رُخَص licence, permit

رَسْمي official (adj.), formal

رِعايَة welfare

رَفَض رَفْض I i/u to refuse, reject

رَفَع رَفْع I a to file, submit (a request etc.)

رَقْم ج أرْقام figure, number

ركّز ه في II to concentrate on

رَمْزي symbolic, token (adj.)

رئيس → رؤساء

رِئاسة\رِياسة chairmanship, directorship

رَئيس ج رُؤَساء chairman, director

رَئيسي principal, key (adj.)

زاد ه\ intr. زيادة I ī to increase

زوّد ب II to supply

زاد see زيادة

سابِقة precedent, precedence

سَبَب ج أسْباب cause

discount rate سِعْر الخَصْم

embassy سِفارة

ambassador سَفير ج سُفَراء

see تركيبة سكّاني

secretary سِكْرِتير

سلسلة ← سلاسل

negative سَلْبي

series سِلْسِلة ج سَلاسِل

authority, see تفويض سُلْطَة

broker سِمْسار ج سَماسِرة

reputation سُمْعة

annual, see ربع سنوي

II to facilitate سهّل ه ل/على

agility سُهولة التَغْيير

(f. adj.) see قائمة سوداء

bad faith سوء النِيّة

see قوّة ,اقتصاد سوق

tourism سيّاحة

policy, politics سيّاسة

see أمّ سيّدة

IQ to dominate سَيْطر على سَيْطرة

partnership شَراكة

(pre)condition	شَرْط ج شُروط
	شريك ← شركاء
company, corporation, firm (n.),	شَرِكة
see أمّ, نقل	
conglomerate	شَرِكة مُتَعَدِّدة الأَنْشِطة
start-up (company)	شَرِكة ناشِئة
	شرط ← شروط
partner	شَريك ج شُرَكاء
co-founder	شَريك مؤَسِّس
grassroot (adj.)	شَعْبي
work, occupation	شُغْل ج أشْغال
II to operate s.t.	شغّل ه
certificate	شَهادة
net(t)	صافٍ
pro bono	لِلصالِح العامّ
correct, right (adj.)	صَحيح
transaction, deal	صَفْقة ج صَفَقات
quality, attribute, characteristic	صِفة
in his capacity as ...	بِصِفَته ...ًا
industry	صِناعة
industrial, see منطقة	صِناعي
International Monetary Fund, IMF	صَنْدوق النَقْد الدُوَلي

ضَبَر ضَبْر I *u* to (place in a) file

ضَبَط ضَبْط I *u/i* to check, control

ضَرورة necessity

طارئ ج طَوارئ contingency, emergency

طبّق ه على II to apply s.t. to s.t.

طَبيعي natural

طرق see تنظيم

طارئ ← طوارئ

طوّر ه II to develop

طويل see مدًى

عاجِل urgent

عادل see تجارة

عادي normal, see غير

عالَمي world (adj.), see منظّمة

عامّ public, general, see اتّفاقيّة, أمين, إنفاق, صالح, مدير

عامِل ج عَوامِل factor (thing)

عائد yield

عَجَز عن عَجْز I *i* to fall short of

عجّل II to expedite

عَدَم مُساوَاة inequality

عربي see جامعة

عُرْف practice (established custom)

عُضْو ج أَعْضاء member

عُضْوِيّة membership

عُطْلة ج عُطَل holiday \sound

قوّة see عظمى (f. comparative adj.)

عَلاقة relation(ship)

عِلْم الإحْصاء statistics

كثيف see عمالة

عَمِل (ه) عَمَل ج أَعْمال I a to do, work, make

عَمَل ج أَعْمال work, labor/labour, see تنظيم

عَمَلي practical

مدير see عمليات

أشغال see عمومي

عَهِد إلى ب عَهْد I a to entrust to s.o. s.t.

عامل ← عوامل

عَوْلَمة globalisation

أخذ see عين

لِغَرَض مُحَدَّد ad hoc

غُرْفة التِجارة chamber of commerce

غَيْر عادي extraordinary (meeting, measure, powers etc.)

فاق فَوْق I ū to exceed

III to negotiate فاوض

period فَتْرة ج فَتَرات

II to inspect فتّش ه

I a to examine, test فَحَص فَحْص ج فُحوص

see نظام فدرالي

chance, opportunity, see انتهز فُرْصة ج فُرَص

branch فَرْع ج فُروع

I a to fail فشِل فشَل

I i to separate فصَل من\بين فصْل

II to prefer فضّل

effective, efficient فَعّال

effectiveness, efficiency فَعّاليّة

bubble فُقّاعة

technical فَنّي

II to delegate (to s.o. s.t.) فوّض إلى\ال ه

black list قائمة سَوْداء

I a to accept قَبِل ه ه قَبول

capacity (to/for) قُدْرة (على)

decision, see اتّخاذ قَرار

II to decide قرّر

division, department قِسْم ج أُقْسام

purpose قَصْد

قصير see مدًى

قِطاع sector

قلّة see احْتكار

قَوْمي national

قُوَّة عُظْمى superpower

قيادة leadership

كامِل complete

كَثيف العَمالة labor/labour intensive

كَساد bust

كَفالة sponsorship

كَفيل ج كُفَلاء sponsor

كلّي see اقتصاد

كمّي see تحليل

كمّيّة quantity

لا رُجوعَ فيه irrevocable

لامُساوَاة inequality

بِلا نَقْض irrevocable

لَجْنة ج لِجان committee, commission, board

لوّث II to pollute

مالِك ج مُلاّك owner

مبدأ ← مبادئ

مُباشِر direct (adj.), immediate

مَبْدأ ج مَبادئ principle

مُتَأَكِّد certain, sure (person)

مُتَبادَل reciprocal

مُتَخَصِّص specialist, specialised

مُتَسَلْسِل serial

شركة متعدّد see

مُتَعَدِّد الأَطْراف multilateral

مُتَعَدِّد الجِنْسِيّات multinational, transnational

مُتَغَيِّر variable (n./adj.)

اقتصاد متقدّم see

مُتَنَوِّع miscellaneous

مُتَوازِن balanced

مُتَوَسِّط average, mean (n./adj.),

medium (adj.), مدّة see

مثّل II to represent

مَجال field, domain

مجموع ← مجاميع

مَجْلِس الإدارة board of directors

مَجْموع ج مَجاميع\sound group

تجارة see محاصيل

مُحْتَمَل probable, potential (adj.)

مدّة , غرض see محدّد

مَحْدود limited, see مُدّة, مسؤولية

مُخاطَرة risk

مُخَطَّط تَنْظيمي organigram(me)

مدير ← مدراء

مَدَني civil, see أشغال, موظّف

مُدّة ج مُدَد period

بِمُدّة ثابِتة fixed-term

بِمُدّة مُتَوَسِّطة medium-term

بِمُدّة مُحَدَّدة\مَحْدودة limited-term

مُدير العَمَلِيَات chief operations officer,

operations manager, COO

مَدًى period, term, range

على مَدًى طَويل long-term

على مَدًى قَصير short-term

مُدير تَنْفيذي chief executive officer, CEO

مُدير ج مُدَراء manager, director

مُدير عامّ general manager,

managing director

مرحلة ← مراحل

مركز ← مراكز

مُرْجأ deferred

مَرْحَلة ج مَراحِل phase

مَرْكَز ج مَراكِز center/centre

مَرْكَزي central(ised)

مَرِن flexible

مُرُونة flexibility, elasticity

مُساءَلة accountability

مُساعَدة aid

مَسْألة ج مَسائل matter

عدم مساواة see

مسألة ← مسائل

مُسْتَشار consultant

مُسْتَوًى level (n.)

مَسَح مَسْح I a to survey

مَسْؤوليّة مَحْدودة limited liability

مُشارَكة partnership

مشروع ← مشاريع

حلّ see , مشكلة ← مشاكل

مُشْتَرَك joint, common

مَشْروط conditional, qualified

مَشْروع ج مَشاريع\sound project

مُشْكِلة ج مَشاكِل\sound problem

مصدر ← مصادر

مصلحة ← مصالح

مَصْدَر ج مَصادِر (re)source

منظّمة see مصدّر

مَصْلَحة ج مَصالِح interest, concern

مُضادّ opposing, counter-

(bid, proposal etc.)

معيار ← معايير

مُعْضِلة problem, see حلّ

مِعْيَار ج مَعايير criterion, norm, standard (n.)

مُغْتَرِب expatriate

مُقابِل in exchange for in cst.

مَقْبول acceptable

مُقيم resident

مكتب ← مكاتب

مَكان ج أماكِن\أمْكِنة place

مَكْتَب ج مَكاتِب office

مَكْتَبي clerical

مالك ← ملاّك

مُلْزِم binding (adj.)

مِلْكي proprietary

تغيير see مناخي

مُناسِب appropriate, opportune

مُناسَبة opportunity, occasion

منصب ← مناصب

منطقة ← مناطق

مُنافِس competitor

مُنافَسة competition

مُناقَصة bid, tender, see أعلن

مَنَح ه ه مَنْح I *a* to grant

مُنْحَنى curve

مُنْشَآت pl. premises, installations

مَنْصِب ج مَناصِب office, post, function

مَنْطِق logic, rationale

مِنْطَقة صِناعِيّة industrial estate

مِنْطَقة مَناطِق area, region

مُنَظَّمة organisation (body)

مُنَظَّمة التِجارة العالَمِيّة World Trade Organisation, WTO

مُنَظَّمة الدُوَل المُصَدِّرة Organisation of Petroleum

للنَفْط (أوْبَيْك) Exporting Countries, OPEC

مُنْفَصِل separate

مُتَقَلِّب volatile

مُنَوَّع miscellaneous

مَهَمَّة ج مَهامّ task, assignment

مورد ← موارد

موعد ← مواعد\مواعيد

مُوَافَقة agreement, consent

مَوْجود available

مَوْرِد ج مَوَارِد resource

مُؤَسِّس founder, see شريك

مُؤَسَّسة foundation, institution, enterprise, firm (n.)

مؤَشِّر index

مُوَظَّف مَدَني\حُكومي civil servant

مَوْعِد ج مَوَاعِد appointment (agreed date/time)

مَوْعِد أخير deadline

مُؤَقَّت temporary, provisional

مَيَّز (بين وَبين) II to distinguish, discriminate, differentiate (between)

شركة ,سوق see ناشئة

اقتصاد see نام

نائِب ج نُوَّاب deputy

نائِب ... deputy ..., vice-... (in cst.)

نَتيجة ج نَتائِج result

نَجَح نَجاح I *a* to succeed

نِزاع conflict

نسَّق II to coordinate

نَصَح (ل ب) نَصْح\نَصيحة I *a* to advise (s.o. on s.t.)

نِظام الإحْتِياطي الفِدِرالي federal reserve system

نِظام ج أَنْظِمة system, regulation

نَظَري theoretical

نَظَريّة theory

نظَّم II to organise

نفَّذ II to execute, fulfil(l)

منظّمة see نفط

نِقابة syndicate

صندوق see نقد

نَقَص عن نَقْص I *u* to fall short of

نَقَض ه نَقْض I *u* to revoke, see لا

نُقْطة ج نُقَط\نِقاط point

نُمُوّ growth

نائب ← نوّاب

نوّع ه II to diversify

نَوْعي specific, see تحليل

نَوْعيّة quality

نيّة ج نَوايا intention, see حسن, سوء \sound

هُبوط slump, fall

هَدَف ج أهْداف goal, target, see إدارة

هُوِيّة identity

هَيْكَل ج هَياكِل structure

هَيْكَل تَنْظيمي organisational chart

هَيْئَة board, commission

جهة see واحد

وافق (ه ه\في\على) III to agree (with s.o. on s.t.)

وجّه (ه إلى\ل) II to direct (s.t. to)

وَحْدة unit

وِزارة ministry

وزير ← وزراء

وزّع II to distribute, allocate

وَزير ج وُزَراء minister

وسيلة ← وسائل

وسّع ه II to expand

وَسيلة ج وَسائل means

وَطَني national

وَظيفة ج وَظائف function

تدرّج see وظيفي

وِفاق agreement, consent

وِقائي protective (in trade), preventive

وَكالة agency

وَكيل ج وُكَلاء agent

وَلّد II to generate

2. DATA & COMMUNICATION

اِتِّصال communication

اتّصل ب VIII to contact/telephone s.o.

آلة إتلاف see

أتلف IV to shred (paper)

أجاب ه\إلى عن\على IV to answer

جهاز إجابة see

تواصل اجتماعي see

جهاز ← أجهزة

نشرة أخبار see

ختم ← أختام

خطأ ← أخطاء

نسخ اِحْتِياطي see

أدخل IV to input, insert

إدْخال بَيَانات data entry

دليل ← أدلّة

سماعة أذن see

أرّخ II to date

أرسل إلى\ل ه IV to send, transmit

خطّ أرضي see

أرفق ب IV to attach to

استرجع X to retrieve (data)

استعلم (٥) عن X to enquire (of s.o.) about

اِسْتِلام receipt (act), see وصل

سرّ ← أسرار

أُسْطُوَانة disk

أشار إلى IV to refer to

إشارة sign, reference, signal

إنترنت see أشياء

أصدر ه IV to issue

قمر see اصطناعي

أعلن IV to announce

اِفْتِراضي virtual, see مساعد, واقع

وحدة see , قرص ← أقراص

ألحق IV to attach, annex, append

إلِكْتْروني electronic, see بريد, موقع, نسخة

آلة device, apparatus

آلة إتْلاف وَرَق (paper-)shredder

آلة طِباعة printer

آلة مَسْح scanner

لوحة ← ألواح

حاسب see آلي

شبكة, عنوان internet, see إنْتِرْنِت

إِنْتِرْنِت الأشْياء internet of things

مذكور آنِفًا see

أوجز ه\في IV to abridge, summarise

ورقة ← أوراق

أوضح IV to elucidate

إيصال receipt (voucher)

أَيْقونة icon

إيمَيْل e-mail

باقة plan

بَرامِج software, ← برنامج pl.

برمج بَرْمَجة IQ to program

بَرْنامَج ج بَرامِج (computer, data) program

بَرْنامَج حاسوب software

بَرْنامَج خَبيث malware

بَرْنامَج مَجّاني freeware

بَريد mail

بَريد إلِكْتْروني e-mail

بَصْمة رَقْمِيّة digital footprint

بَطّارِيّة battery

بِطاقة card

بُعْد see تحكّم, وصول

بَنْك الطاقة power bank

بَوّابة portal

data, see إدخال ,تحليل ,جدول, بَيَانات
قاعدة, معالجة, معدّل

III to follow (events, information, تابع
s.o. on social media)

roaming (n.) تَجْوَال

upgrading تَحْدِيث

remote control تَحَكُّم عن بُعْد

analysis تَحْلِيل بَيَانات

analytical تَحْلِيلِي

upload تَحْمِيل

call forwarding تَحْوِيل المُكالَمة

frequency تَرَدُّد

see نظام تشغيل

encryption تَشْفِير

V to browse تصفّح

see جهاز تصوير

application تَطْبِيق

comment تعليق ج تعاليق\sound

instructions تَعْلِيمات

feedback تَغْذِية راجِعة

presentation تَقْدِيم

tweet تَغْرِيد

1Q to televise تلفز no vb. n.

تِلِفِزْيُون television

تلفن ل\إلى IQ to telephone no vb. n.

تِليفون telephone

تَنْزيل download

تَوَاصُل اِجْتِماعي social media

جهاز توجيه see

جَدْوَل ج جَداوِل schedule, table

جَدْوَل بَيَانات spreadsheet

جُمْلة ج جُمَل sentence

جِهاز إجابة answering machine

جِهاز ج أجْهِزة device, apparatus

جِهاز تَصْوِير (photo)copier

جِهاز تَوْجيه router

جِهاز لَوْحي tablet

جِهاز نِداء beeper, paging device

هاتف see جوّال

مكَّونات ,برنامج حاسوب see

حاسِب آلي computer

حَذَف حَذْف I i to delete

حرّر II to edit

حَفِظ حِفْظ I a to save (data)

حلّل II to analyse

حَوْسَبة سَحابيّة cloud computing

خادِم ج خُدّام server

برنامج see خبيث

خَتْم ج أَخْتام seal

خَتَم I i to seal خَتْم

خادم ← خدّام

خَطّ أَرْضي landline

خَطّ ج خُطوط (telephone etc.) line/extension

خَطأ ج أَخْطاء error

خطّط II to plan

خُطّة ج خُطَط plan, scheme

خطّ ← خطوط

دِراسة study

دَرْدَشة chat

دَعَم I a to back up دَعْم

وحدة see دفع

دَليل ج أَدِلّة directory

ذاكِرة memory

ذَكَر I u to mention ذِكْر

هاتف see ذكي

راجع ه III to review, revert/refer to,
تغذية see

سماعة see رأس

راقب III to inspect, censor, check

رَدًّا على in reply to

رِسالة ج رَسائل letter, note, message

رِسالة شارِحة explanatory letter

رِسالة نَصِّيّة text message

رسالة ← رَسائل

رَسْم ج رُسوم drawing, graph, chart

رَقْمي digital, see بَصمة, معرفة

رَمْز ج رُموز sign, symbol, code

مذكور سابِقًا see

سجّل II to register, record

سحابي see حوسبة

سِرّ ج أَسْرار secret (n.)

سِرّي secret (adj.), confidential

سلكي see لا

سَماعة أُذْن earphone

سَماعة لِلرّأس headphone

شاحِن charger

شارح see رسالة

شاشة screen, monitor

شَبَكة ج شِباك network sound\

خارج شَبَكة الإِنْتِرْنِت offline

على شَبَكة الإِنْتِرْنِت online

شَبَكة لاسِلْكيّة wi-fi

شَحَن شَحْن I *a* to charge (electrically)

شَريحة ج شَرائح chip

صَفْحة ج صَفَحات page, sheet

محرّك ,قرص صلب see محرّك

يفعّل see صوت

صَوْتي voice-activated, see مكالمة

طابِع ج طَوابِع stamp (impression/paper)

طاقة see بنك

طِباعة printer, see آلة

طَبَع طَبْع I *a* to print

طابِع → طوابِع

ظَرْف ج ظُروف envelope

عالَج III to process

عِبارة expression, phrase

عبّر عن II to express

عدّل II to amend

عَرْض ج عُرُوض display

عَلامة (computing) label

عُنْوان ج عَناوِين address

عُنْوان مَوْقِع الإنْتِرْنِت uniform/universal resource locator, URL

غرّد II to tweet

(tele)fax   فاكْس

see نصّ   فائق

cyberspace   فَضاء مَعْلوماتي

index, table of contents   فِهْرِس ج فَهارِس

virus   فَيْروس

database   قاعِدة بَيَانات

disk   قُرْص ج أقْراص

hard disk, see محرّك   قُرْص صُلْب

floppy disk   قُرْص مَرِن

satellite (n.)   قَمَر اِصْطِناعي

channel   قَناة ج قَنَوات

I i to disclose   كَشَف ه\عن كَشْف

word   كَلِمة

computer   كَمْبْيُوتَر

radio/wireless (adj.), see شبكة   لا سِلْكي

I a to paste to   لَصِق ب لَصْق

(notice- etc.) board sound\   لَوْحة ج ألْوَاح

see جهاز   لوحي

fair copy   مُبَيَّضة

see هاتف   متحرّك

browser   مُتَصَفِّح

see هويّة   متكلّم

see برنامج   مجّاني

مُجَلَّد folder

مُحَرِّك قُرْص صُلْب hard disk drive

مَحْظُور blocked

مَحْفُوظات archives

مَدْخَل input

مُدَوِّن blogger

مُدَوَّنة blog

مُذَكِّرة memorandum

مَذْكُور (سابِقًا\آنِفًا) (afore)mentioned

مرجع ← مراجع

مُراسَلة correspondence

تغذية see مرتدّ

مَرْجِع ج مَراجِع reference (thing referred to)

قرص see مرن

مكالمة see مرئي

مُساعِد اِفْتِراضي virtual assistant

مُسْتَنَد document

آلة see مسح

مُسَوَّدة draft, proof/rough copy

مُعالَجة المُعْطَيات\البَيانات data-processing

مُعالَجة النُصوص word-processing

مُعَدَّل نَقْل البَيانات bandwidth

مَعْرِفة رَقْميّة digital literacy

data, see معالجة	مُعْطَيَات
information	مَعْلومات pl.
see فضاء	معلوماتي
see تحويل	مكالمة
voice call	مُكالَمة صَوْتيّة
video call	مُكالَمة مَرْئيّة
hardware	مُكَوَّنات حاسوب
file (n.)	مِلَفّ
forum	مُنْتَدًى
see عنوان	موقع
website	مَوْقِع إِلِكْتْروني
window	نافِذة
paging, see جهاز	نِداء
I a to copy	نَسَخ نَسْخ
نسخة ← نسخ	
backup	نَسْخ اِحْتِياطي
soft copy	نُسْخة إِلِكْتْرونيّة
copy/duplicate (of)	نُسْخة ج نُسَخ (عن)
hard/paper copy	نُسْخة وَرَقيّة
I u to publish; to post (social media)	نَشَر نَشْر
bulletin, circular, publication	نَشْرة
newsletter	نَشْرة أَخْبار
hypertext	نَصّ فائق

text, see معالجة نَصّ ج نُصوص

see رسالة نصّي

operating system نِظام تَشْغِيل

see هاتف نقّال

I u to click (on) نَقَر (ه) نَقْر

see معدّل نقل

model/specimen (n.), نَموذَج ج نَماذِج\sound

form (document)

telephone هاتِف ج هَوَاتِف

mobile phone هاتِف جَوَّال\نقّال\مُتَحَرِّك

smart phone هاتِف ذَكي

هاتف ⟶ هواتف

caller identification/identity هُوِيّة المُتَكَلِّم

virtual reality واقِع اِفْتِراضي

supporting document وَثيقة ج وَثائق

disk drive وَحْدة دَفْع أقْراص

paper (collective), see آلة وَرَق

paper وَرَقة ج أوْراق

see نسخة ورقي

receipt (voucher) وَصْل اِسْتِلام

remote access وُصول عن بُعْد

II to (counter)sign وقّع

voice-activated يُفَعَّل بِالصَوْت

3. FINANCE

credit, see بطاقة	اِئْتِمان
fee, rate, pay, wage	أجْر ج أُجور
gross (n./adj.)	إجْمالي
gross national product, GNP	إجْمالي الناتِج القَوْمي
gross domestic product, GDP	إجْمالي الناتِج المَحَلِّي
see عملة	أجنبي
أجور ← أجر	
reserve (n./adj.)	اِحْتياطي
wealth management	إدارة الثَرْوَات
see حساب	اِدّخار
أرباح ← ربح	
capital gains	أرْباح رأْسْماليّة\رأُس المال
appreciation	اِرْتِفاع القيمة
VIII to increase	ارتفع
أرصدة ← رصيد	
credit crunch	أزْمة الإئْتِمان
investment, see صناديق, عرض,	اِسْتِثْمار
فترة, محفظة	
X to invest	استثمر
maturity	اِسْتِحْقاق

استردّ X to recover (money)

اِسْتِرْداد نَقْدي cashback

استفاد X to capitalise

استلم VIII to receive

سعر ← أسعار

قيمة see اسمي

سهم ← أسهم

سوق ← أسواق

أُصول .pl assets

اِعْتِماد credit

اِعْتِماد مالي fund

عدد ← أعداد

إعْفاء ضَرِيبي tax exemption

مسرّع see أعمال

أفلس IV to be(come) bankrupt

اقترض VIII to borrow

اِقْتِصاد economy, economics

أغلق IV to close

جهاز see آلي

صندوق see آمن

غسيل see أموال

خفض expenditure, see إنْفاق

إنْفاق عامّ public spending

إنْقاذ bailout

اِنْكِماش deflation

أودع IV to deposit

صندوق see إيداع

إيراد yield, return

بطاقة ,أزمة see ائتمان

فائدة see بسيط

بِطاقة اِئْتِمان credit card

بِطاقة خَصْم debit card

بَنْك ج بُنوك bank

بَنْك مَرْكَزي central bank

بنك → بنوك

بورْصة stock exchange

تَثْبيت سِعْر العُمْلة currency peg

تَحْليل التَكْلِفة والمَنْفَعة cost-benefit analysis

تَخْفيف عِبء الدَيْن debt relief

تَخْفيض القيمة devaluation

منصّة → تداول

تَدَفُّق رأْس المال capital flow

تراجع VI to retract, recede

تَضَخُّم inflation

تَعْويم floating

تَقَشُّف austerity

تَقَلُّب (السوق) (market) volatility

تَقْييم المَخاطِر risk assessment

تَكْلِفة cost, see تحليل

تَمْويل funding

تَمْويل جَماعي crowd-funding

تَنْويع diversification

توفير see حساب

ثابِت fixed (assets, prices, income),

see سند

ثَرْوَة wealth, see إدارة

جارٍ see حساب

جمَّد ه II to freeze

جماعي see تمويل

جِهاز الصَرّاف الآلي automated teller machine, ATM,

cash dispenser

جِنَيْه pound (£)

حاضن see مستثمر

حامِل bearer

حرّة see سوق

حِساب account, calculation, see

كشف, قيّد, دفتر

حِساب التَوْفير\الإدِّخار savings account

حِساب جارٍ checking/current account

حِساب وَدائع deposit account

حُقوق المِلْكية equity

حَوَالة مَصْرِفيّة banker's draft

حوّل II to transfer

خارج see نقل

خَزِينة ج خَزائن safe (n.), treasury

خَسِر ه خَسارة ج خَسائر I a to lose

خصّص ل ه II to appropriate (funds etc.) for

خصم see بطاقة

خَفْض الإنْفاق spending cut

دائِن creditor

دَخْل income, see سند, ضريبة

دِرْهَم ج دَراهِم dirham

دَفْتَر (حِساب) (account) book, ledger

دَفْتَر شيكات check/cheque book

دَفْع (ل\إلى ه) دَفْع I a to pay

دَفْع ج مَدْفوعات payment

دقّق II to audit

دولار dollar

دولي see بنك, صندوق

دينار ← دنانير

دَيْن ج دُيُون debt, see تخفيف

دينار ج دَنانير dinar

دين ← ديون

رأْس المال see أرباح, تدفّق

رأْس المال\رأْسْمال capital (n.), see هروب

رأْس مال المُجازَفة venture capital

رأْسْمالي capital (adj.), capitalist, see أرباح

رَبِح (مِن) رِبْح I *a* to profit (from)

رِبْح ج أرْباح profit, gain, interest, see هامش

رَسْم ج رُسوم charge, fee

رَصيد ج أرْصِدة balance, available funds

رقمي see عملة

رُكود recession

رَهْن عَقاري mortgage

رِيال rial, riyal

رئيس المُحاسَبة chief accountant

سَحَب سَحْب I *a* to withdraw (money)

سَحْب على المَكْشوف overdraft

سلّد II to defray, amortise

سرّع II to accelerate

سِعْر ج أسْعار price, see تثبيت

سِعْر الصَرْف exchange rate

سِلْسِلة الكُتَل blockchain

سلّف ه ه II to advance, lend

سَنَد bond, security

سَنَد الدَخْل الثابِت fixed income bond

سوق see سوداء (f. adj.)

سوق ج أسْواق .f market, see تقلّب

سوق حُرّة free market

سوق سَوْداء black market

سوق ناشِئة emerging market

سوقي see قيمة

سَهْم ج أسْهُم share, equity

سوّى ه II to settle (debt, dispute etc.)

شرائي see قوّة

شَرِكة ناشئة start-up (company)

شيك see دفتر

شيك مُسَطَّر crossed check/cheque

صافٍ net(t) (adj.)

صَرّاف teller, see جهاز

صَرْف exchange, see سعر

صَكّ ج صُكوك certificate of investment

صَناديق اِسْتِثْمار مُشْتَرَك mutual funds

صَنْدوق الإيداع الآمِن safe(ty) deposit box

ضريبة ← ضرائب

ضَريبة الدَخْل income tax

ضَريبة ج ضَرائب tax

ضَريبة على القيمة المُضافة value-added tax, VAT

إعفاء see ضريبي

ضَمان bond, security, guarantee

عائد ج عَوائد\sound dividend

إنفاق see عامّ

تخفيف see عبء

عَجْز deficit

عجّل II to accelerate

عَدَد ج أعْداد number

عدّل ه II to adjust

عَرْض الاسْتِثْمار investment deck/spread

عَرْض ج عُروض bid, tender

رهن see عقاري

عُمْلة currency, see تثبيت

عُمْلة أجْنَبيّة foreign currency

عُمْلة رَقْميّة digital currency

عُمْلة مُشَفّرة cryptocurrency

ميزانية see عمومي

II to reimburse (for) عوّض ه (من\عن)

عائد ← عوائد

strongroom, vault غُرْفة مُحَصَّنة

money laundering غَسيل أمْوال

invoice فاتورة

simple interest فائدة بَسيطة

interest, see قرض فائدة ج فَوَائد

compound interest فائدة مُرَكَّبة

surplus فائِض

tenor فَتْرة الاِسْتِثْمار

فائدة ← فوائد

II to evaluate (at) قدّر (ب)

loan قَرْض ج قُروض

soft/low-interest loan قَرْض مُنْخَفَض الفائدة

قرض ← قروض

accounts department قِسْم المُحاسَبة

see إجمالي قومي

purchase/purchasing power قُوّة شِرائيّة

II to debit s.o. with s.t. قيّد على ه

II to credit (an account) with قيّد ه (لِحِساب)

قيمة ← قيم

to evaluate (at) قيّم (ب)

قيمة اِسْميّة face value

قيمة سُوقيّة market value

value, see ارتفاع, تخفيض, ضريبة قيمة ج قِيَم

see سلسلة كتل

(bank/financial) statement كَشْف حِساب

I u to bail s.o. out كَفَل ه كَفالة

II to cost (s.o.) s.t. كلّف (ه) ه

irrevocable بِلا نَقْض

lira ليرة

per cent بِالمِائة

see هروب, رأس, تدفّق أرباح مال

financial, see مدير, اعتماد, مالي

مشتقات

amount مَبْلَغ ج مَبالِغ

amount due مَبْلَغ مُسْتَحَقّ

arrears مُتَأَخِّرات

see رأس مجازفة

total مَجْموع

accountant مُحاسِب

accounting, accountancy, مُحاسَبة

see قسم, رئيس

see غرفة محصّن

مَحْفَظة الاسْتِثْمارات investment portfolio

مَحلّي see إجمالي

مَخاطر see تقييم

مدفوعات ← دفع

مُدير مالي chief financial officer, CFO,

finance manager

مَدين debit, debtor

مَردود yield, return

مركّب see فائدة

مركزي see بنك

مُساهِم shareholder

مُسْبَق advance (adj.)

مُسْتَثْمِر investor

مُسْتَثْمِر حاضِن incubator

مستحقّ see مبلغ

مُسَرِّع الأعْمال accelerator

مسطّر see شيك

مشترك see صناديق

مُشْتَقّات ماليّة derivatives

مشقّر see عملة

مَصْرِف ج مَصارِف bank

مَصْرِفي banking (adj.), see حوالة

مضاف see ضريبة

مُعامَلة transaction, deal

مُكافأة bonus

مَكْشوف uncovered, overdrawn

(amount, account), see سحب

مُلْكيّة property

مِلْكيّة ownership, see حقوق

مُمْتَلَكات .pl property

مُناقَصة tender

منخفض see قرض

مِنَصّة تَداوُل exchange platform

مَنْفَعة benefit, see تحليل

ميزان ← موازين

موّل II to finance, fund

ميزان ج مَوَازين balance

ميزانيّة budget

ميزانيّة عُمُوميّة balance sheet

بِالمِئة per cent

ناتج see اجمالي

ناشئة see شركة, سوق

نِسْبة ج نِسَب rate

نَفَقة expenditure

نَقْد ج نُقود cash, (pl.) money, see صندوق

نقض see لا

نقد ← نقود

نقدي see استرداد

نُقْطة ج نُقَط point

نَقَل ه إلى الخارج نَقْل I u to offshore s.t. to

هامِش رِبْح profit margin

هُروب رأس المال capital flight

ودائع see حساب

وَديعة ج وَدائع deposit

يِنّ yen

يورو euro

4. INSURANCE

أجَّر	II to let/lease out
أُجْرة	rent
أُجْرة العَرْض	ground rent
إحالة	referral
أحكام see متوافق	
اِخْتِياري	optional
أخطار ⟵ خطر, see تأمين	
ادّعَ	VIII to claim
أرباح see مشاركة	
بِأرْباح	with profits (policy etc.)
أساسي see مستفيد	
استأجر	X to hold/take on lease
استبدال see قيمة, سعر	
اِسْتِثْناء	exclusion
استفاد (من)	X to benefit (from)
استهلاك see بلى	
اِسْتِهْلاك عادي\مَعْقول	fair wear and tear
اِسْتِثْناف	appeal
إسلامي see تكافل, متوافق	
إصابة	injury

إصابة صِناعيّة industrial injury

صاحب ← أصحاب

اِصْطِدام collision

أصلح ه\ب IV to repair

أضْرار جَسَديّة bodily injury

تأمين see, ضرر ← أضرار

إعادة تَنْصيب reinstatement

إعاقة disability

اقتطع VIII to deduct

قسط ← أقساط

حدّ see أقصى

اِلْتِزام (ب) obligation, liability (for)

إلْزامي compulsory

ضمان see أمانة

لا غ see أمر

ملك ← أملاك

أمّن II to insure, assure

أمّن على II to underwrite

تاريخ see انتهاء

أهْليّة eligibility

أهمل IV to neglect

إهْمال مُساعِد contributory negligence

تأمين see بحري

سيّارة see بديل

(insurance) policy بوليصة ج بَوَالِص

named policy بوليصة مُعَيَّنة

termination date تاريخ اِنْتِهاء

insurance, assurance, تَأْمين

see خبير, قابل, وثيقة

تكافل see تأمين إسلامي

marine insurance تَأْمين بَحْري

travel insurance تَأْمين السَفَر

personal insurance تَأْمين شَخْصي

damage insurance تَأْمين ضدّ الأضْرار

all-risks insurance تَأْمين ضدّ جَميع الأخْطار

fire insurance تَأْمين ضدّ الحَريق

accident insurance تَأْمين ضدّ الحَوَادِث

life assurance تَأْمين على الحَيَاة

theft insurance تَأْمين ضدّ السَرِقة

health insurance تَأْمين صِحّي

medical insurance تَأْمين طِبّي

third-party insurance تَأْمين ضدّ الغَيْر

flood insurance تَأْمين ضدّ الفَيَضان

vehicle insurance تَأْمين مَرْكَبات

تَأْمِين مُشْتَرَك co-insurance

تَأْمِين مُوَحَّد unified insurance

تَخْرِيب malicious act

تَسْوِية settlement

تَصادُم collision

تَصْرِيح declaration

تَضَرُّر damage

تَعاوُنِي mutual (assurance, policy etc.)

تَعْرِيفة tariff

تَعْوِيض compensation, see قسم

تَعْوِيضِي compensatory

تَغْطِية عالَمِيّة worldwide coverage

تَفْوِيض authorisation

تَفْوِيض مُسْبَق pre-authorisation

حسب تَقْدِير at discretion (of)

تَكافُل (تَأْمِين إِسْلامي) *takāful* (Islamic insurance)

تلف see بلى

تنازل (ل) عن III to waive (in favor/favour of)

تنصيب see إعادة

ثالث see طرف

ثَمَّن II to appraise

جسدي see أضرار

جميع see تأمين

حادِث ج حَوَادِث accident

حادِث صِناعي industrial accident

حَدّ أقْصى excess (n.)

حَدّ قانوني legal limit

تأمين, fire, see حَريق ج حَرائق

خبير see حسابات

حَقّ السِرِّيّة الطِبّية medical confidentiality

حِماية الدَخْل income protection

تأمين, حادث see حوادث

مدى, تأمين life, see حَياة ج حَيَوات

خَبير حِسابات شُؤون actuary
التَأْمين

خَسارة ج خَسائر damage, loss

خَسارة كُلّيّة total loss

خسارة خسائر

خصّص ه\ل ه II to assign to

خَطَر ج أخْطار risk

حماية see دخل

دَفْعة سَنَوِيّة annuity

نظام see سداد

سدّد II to settle, defray, discharge

سَرَق (٥\من) ه سَرِقة I *i* to steal (from)

تأمين see سرقة

حقّ see سرّيّة

سَطْو burglary

سِعْر الإسْتِبْدال replacement cost

تأمين see سفر

فترة see سماح

سِمْسار ج سَماسِرة broker

دفعة see سنوي

سَيّارة بَديلة replacement car

شامِل comprehensive

تأمين see شخصي

شَرْح المَزايا explanation of benefits, EOB

متوافق see شريعة

شَكْوى ج شَكاوى grievance

شَهادة مِلْكِيّة certificate of title

خبير see شؤون

صَاحِب ج أصْحاب (property) owner, (policy) holder

تأمين see صحّي

حادث, إصابة see صناعي

ضَرَر ج أضْرار damage

ضَمان الأمانة fidelity guarantee

ضَمِن ل ه ضَمان I a to guarantee

طارئ ج طَوَارئ contingency

حقّ , تأمين see طِبّي

طَرَف ثالِث third party

طوارِئ see طريق

طلَب طلَب I u to claim, apply for

طارئ ← طوارئ

طَوارِئ على الطَريق roadside assistance

بلى , استهلاك see عادي

تغطية see عالَمي

عَجْز كُلّي total disablement

أُجرة see عرض

مرض see عضال

عَقار premises, (piece of) real estate

عُمُولة commission, brokerage

نفقات see عودة

عوّض (من\عن) II to compensate (for), indemnify (against)

تأمين third party, see غَيْر

فاتورة مُفَصَّلة itemised invoice

فَتْرة سَماح grace period

فَقَد ه ه فَقْد I i to lose

فَقْد loss

تأمين see ,فَيَضان flood

قابِل لِلتَأْمين insurable

مسؤوليّة ,حدّ قانوني see

قِسْط ج أَقْساط premium

قِسْم التَعْوِيضات claims department

قَطْرُ المَرْكَبة towing

قيمة الإسْتِبْدال replacement value

كارِثة ج كَوَارِث disaster

عجز ,خسارة كلّي see

كارثة ← كوارث

لاغٍ وَكَأَمْرٍ لَم يَكُن null and void

مسؤولية مادَّي\مالي see

مَبالِغ مُقْتَطَعة deductions

مُتَوافِق مع أَحْكام Shariah-compliant
الشَريعة الإسْلاميّة

مُثَمِّن appraiser

مُدَّعٍ claimant

مسؤوليّة مدني see

لِمَدَى الحَيَاة whole-life (adj.)

مَرَض عُضال terminal disease

مركبة see تأمين, قطر

مزايا see شرح

مساعد see إهمال

تفويض, see prior, مسبق

مُسْتَأْجِر tenant, lessee

مُسْتَفيد أساسي primary beneficiary

مُسْتَفيد مَشْروط contingent beneficiary

مَسْؤُول (عن) responsible/liable (for)

مَسْؤوليّة\مَسْئُوليّة (عن) liability (for)

مَسْؤوليّة\مَسْئُوليّة قانونيّة legal liability

مَسْؤوليّة\مَسْئُوليّة مادّيّة\ماليّة financial liability

مَسْؤوليّة\مَسْئُوليّة مَدَنيّة civil liability

مشترك see تأمين, وثيقة

مُشارَكة في الأرْباح participation in profits

مشروط see مستفيد

مُعال legal dependant/dependent

مُعَدَّل rate

معقول see استهلاك

معيّن see بوليصة

مفصّل see فاتورة

مقتطع see مبالغ

مُكافَأة bonus

مَلَك مُلْك\مِلْك I i to own

مِلْك ج أُمْلاك property (thing owned)

شهادة ملكيّة see

مَنْفَعة ج مَنافِع benefit

مُوافقة consent

تأمين مو حّد see

مُؤَمَّن insured (thing)

مُؤَمِّن insurer

مُؤَمَّن عليه insured (person)

ناتِج (عن) resulting (from), consequent (upon)

نِسْبة ج نِسَب rate

نِظام سَداد reimbursement

نَفَقات العَوْدة إلى الوَطَن repatriation expenses

وَثيقة تَأْمين insurance policy

وَثيقة مُشْتَرَكة joint policy

وَسيط ج وُسَطاء broker

نفقات وطن see

وَكيل ج وُكَلاء agent

لا غٍ يكن see

يَوْمي per diem (benefit, allowance)

5. LAW & CONTRACT

أبطل IV to annul

اِتِّفاق agreement (action/document)

اِتِّفاق شَرَف gentlemen's agreement

اتّفق مع علي VIII to agree with s.o. on s.t.

اِتِّهام impeachment

اتّهم (ب) VIII to accuse (of)

إثْبات evidence

أثبت IV to prove

إجْباري compulsory

إجْراءات proceedings

إجْلاء eviction

اِحْتِيال fraud

اِحْتِيالي fraudulent

محكمة see أحداث

حكم ← أحكام

أحْكام وَشُروط terms and conditions

دائرة see اختصاص

اختلس VIII to embezzle

اِخْتِياري optional

أخلّ ب IV to infringe, violate

إخْلال بِالعَقْد	breach of contract
ادّع	VIII to allege
دليل ← أدلّة	
الموقِّع أدناه	see
استأنف (ه)	X to appeal (against)
استجْوَب	X to cross-examine
تاريخ استحقاق	see
محكمة اسْتِئْناف	appeal, see
اسْمي	nominal
إشاعة	hearsay (n.)
أصدر	IV to pronounce
طرف ← اطراف	
اعْتِراف	confession
إفادة	deposition
افترى على	VIII to slander
إقْرار	affidavit
جريمة إلكتروني	see
أمْر أوَامِر	warrant
أمْر حُضُور	subpoena, summons
أمْر قضائي	injunction
ملك ← أملاك	
غسيل أموال	see

انسحاب see شرط

تاريخ اِنْقِضاء expiry, see

انقضى VII to expire

إنْكار repudiation

إهانة المَحْكَمة contempt of court

أهْليّة competence

أهمل IV to neglect, fail to fulfil(l)

أمر ← أوامر

أوْجب على ه IV to impose on s.o. s.t.

وصي ← أوصياء

يمين ← أيمان

باطِل null, void

بَنْد ج بُنود clause

بيع see عقد

تاريخ الإسْتِحْقاق due date

تاريخ اِنْقِضاء expiry date

تأليف see حق

علامة ,قانون تجاري see

تَجْريم النَفْس self-incrimination

تَجَسُّس صِناعي industrial espionage

تَحْقيق inquest

تَحْكيم arbitration

تَسْوِيّة وُدِّيّة amicable settlement

تَصْفِيّة liquidation

تَعارُض مَصالِح conflict of interests

تَعْوِيض compensation, damages

تُهْمة ج تُهَم charge, indictment

تواطأ (على) VI to collude (in)

توسّط ل (ب\بين\في) V to mediate for (between/in)

توقّف على V to be dependent/conditional on

توقّف عن V to suspend, discontinue

تَوْكِيل رَسْمي power of attorney

شريك جرم see

جَريمة إلِكْتْرونيّة e-crime, cyber crime

شرط جزائي see

دعوى جماعي see

في حالة in (the) case of (in cst.)

حَجَز ه\على حَجْز I u/i to impound

حَجْز custody

حَجْز (على) distraint (of), see حق

حلّد II to define

حَصانة immunity

حَصْري exclusive

أمر حضور see

حَقّ ج حُقوق (في)	right (n.) (to/of)
حَقّ التَّأْليف وَالنَشْر	copyright
حَقّ حَجْز	lien
الْحَقّ عليه	he is (in the) wrong
الْحَقّ معه	he is (in the) right
حقيقة ← حقائق	
حقّ ← حقوق	
حُقُوق مَدَنِيّة	civil rights
حَقيقة ج حَقائق	truth
حَكَم على حُكْم	I u to judge, give judgment on
حُكْم ج أَحْكام	judgment, ruling
حلّف	II to swear in
حِنْث بِالَيَمين	perjury
محاكمة see خاطئ	
خالف	III to infringe, violate
شاهد see خبير	
عق see خدمة	
خِلاف	dispute
دائرة اِخْتِصاص	jurisdiction
دَحْض	rebuttal
دَعا دَعْوَة	I u to summon
دَعْوَى ج دَعاوَى	case, lawsuit , see نظر

دَعْوَى جَماعيّة	class action
دَلّ بِشَهادة (ب\أنّ) دَليل	I *u* to testify (to/that)
دَليل ج أدِلّة	evidence
دَليل ظَرْفي	circumstantial evidence
رِبًا	usury
رَدّ رَدّ ج رُدود	I *u* to dismiss (a case, appeal etc.)
رسمي see وكالة, توكيل	
رَمْزي	nominal
سابِقة	precedent
سريان see مدّة	
سوّى	II to settle
شاهِد خَبير	expert witness
شاهِد ج شُهود	witness
شاهِد عَيان	eyewitness
شَرْط ج شُروط	(pre-)condition, clause
بِشَرْط\على شَرْط (أنْ)	on condition (that) or in cst.
شَرْط اِنْسِحاب	escape clause
شَرْط جَزائي	penalty clause
شَرْعي	valid, lawful
شَرْعيّة	validity, legitimacy
شرف see اتفاق	
شَريك ← شركاء	

شَرِكة ذات مَسْؤوليّة limited liability company
مَحْدودة

شَرِكة مُساهِمة joint stock company

شروط ← شرط, see أحكام

شَريك ج شُرَكاء (في الجُرْم) accessory (in the offence)

شَفافيّة transparency

شَفَهي verbal

شَفَوي oral

شَكْلاً وَمَوْضوعًا in form and content/substance

شَهادة testimony, see دلّ

شَهَد (ب\أنّ) شَهادة I a to testify (to/that)

شهّر ب II to libel

شاهد ← شهود

صاحِب عَقار landlord

صادر III to seize, confiscate

صَحيح true, correct

مَحكمة صغير see صغير

تَجسس see صناعي

عقد see صيانة

ضَبَط ضَبْط I i/u to regulate

ضَحيّة victim

ضَمان warranty

ضِمْني implicit

طَرَف ج أطْراف party

طَعَن على\في طَعْن I u/a to libel s.o.

قابل see طعن

دليل see ظرفي

ظُروف مُخَفَّفة mitigating/extenuating circumstances

ظُروف مُشَدِّدة aggravating circumstances

محكمة, كاتب see عدل

عرقلة see عدالة

عادِل equitable, fair

عَدْل justice, see محكمة

عَرْقَلة العَدالة obstruction of justice

عِقابي punitive

صاحب see عقار

عَقْد بَيْع sales contract

عَقْد خِدْمة service contract

عَقْد صِيانة maintenance contract

عَقْد ج عُقود contract, see إخلال

عَقْد عَمَل employment contract

عُقوبة sanctions

عقد ← عقود

عَلامة تِجاريّة trade mark

محكمة see عليا (f. comparative adj.)

عمل see محكمة, قانون, عقد

عيان see شاهد

غَرامة fine (n.), penalty

غرّم II to fine

غَسيل أمْوَال money laundering

فدرالي see محكمة

فَسَخ فَسْخ I *a* to annul, rescind

فِقْرة clause

فكري see ملكية

غير قابِل لِلطَعْن irrevocable

قابِل لِلمُناقَشة negotiable

قاصِر minor

قاضٍ ج قُضاة judge

قاضى III to sue

قاعَة مَحْكَمة courtroom

قانون ج قَوَانين law

قانون تِجاري commercial law

قانون العَمَل labor/labour law

قانوني legal

قاهر see قوة

قَرْصَنة	hacking, piracy
قاضٍ ← قضاة	
أمر see قضائي	
محكمة see قضايا	
قَضيّة ج قَضايَا	case, lawsuit
قانون ← قوانين	
قُوَّة قاهِرة	force majeure
كاتِب عَدْل	notary public
كاذِب	false
كَفالة	bail
لا غٍ	null, void
مادّة ج مَوادّ	article
مالِك	owner
مُبَلِّغ (عن المُخالِفات)	whistle-blower
محكمة ← محاكِم	
مُحاكَمة خاطئة	mistrial
مُحامٍ	lawyer, attorney
شركة see ,مَحْدود	fixed, definitive, see
قاعة , إهانة see ,مَحْكمة ج مَحاكِم	lawcourt, see
مَحْكمة الأَحْداث	juvenile court
مَحْكمة الاِسْتِئْناف	court of appeal
مَحْكمة العَدْل العُلْيا	high/supreme court
مَحْكمة العَمَل	labour/labor court

مَحْكَمة فِدِراليّة federal court

مَحْكَمة القَضايَا الصَغيرة small claims court, petty sessions

هيئة see محلف

مُخادِع swindler

مُخاصِم adversary, litigant

مبلّغ see مخالفات

ظروف see مخفّف

مُدَّع plaintiff, petitioner

مُدَّعَى عليه respondent, defendant

مَدَني civil (law, case), see حقوق

مُدّة سَرَيَان period of validity

مُذْنِب guilty

شركة see مساهم

شركة see مسؤوليّة

ظروف see مشدّد

مَشْروط conditional

مُصادَرة seizure, confiscation

مَصاريف costs

تعارض see مصالح

مُعَيَّن definite, specific

مُقاضاة litigation

مَقْصود intentional

مُلْحَق appendix, rider

مُلْزِم (على) binding (upon)

مِلْك ج أَمْلاك estate

مِلْكِيّة فِكْرِيّة intellectual property

قابل see مناقشة

مادّة ← مَوادّ

المُوَقِّع أَدْناه the undersigned

مَوْثوق بِه credible

شكلاً see موضوعًا

مُؤَهَّل competent

نازع ه ه III to dispute with s.o. s.t.

حق see نشر

نَظَر في دَعْوَى hearing

نفّذ II to fulfil(l), execute, enforce

تجريم see نفس

نِهائي final, irrevocable

هُوِيّة identity

هَيْئة مُحَلَّفين jury

وثّق II to notarise

وَحيد exclusive

تسوية see ودي

وَصي ج أَوْصياء guardian

وَكالة رَسْمِيّة power of attorney

يَمين ج أَيْمان oath, see حنث

6. RESEARCH & PRODUCTION

بئر ← آبار

اِبْتِكار innovation

بحث ← أبحاث

اِتِّفاقيّة تَحْسين productivity agreement
الإنْتاجيّة

إجْراءات السَلامة safety measures

جهاز ← أجْهِزة pl. equipment,

اِخْتِبار experiment

اِخْتِباري experimental

اختبر VIII to test

اِخْتِراع invention, see براءة

اِخْتِصاصي بِالكَهْرَباء electrician

استبدل ه (ب) X to replace (with s.t.)

اِسْتِدامة sustainability

اِسْتْراتيجيّة strategy

استعان بِمَصْدَر خارِجي X to outsource

سماد ← أسمِدة

اصطنع VIII to synthesise

اِقْتِصاد المَعْرِفة knowledge economy

آلة device, machine, instrument

آلي	mechanical
أَلْياف ضَوْئِيّة	fiber/fibre optics
أمان	safety
اِمْتِياز	concession, franchise
إنْتاج	production, see محطّة
إنْتاج بِالجُمْلة	mass/bulk production
إنْتاجيّة	productivity, see اتّفاقية, حملة,
مفاوضة	
أنتج	IV to produce
انفجر	VII to explode intr.
مادّة	see أوّلي
بِتْرَوْل	petroleum
بَحَثَ (ه\عن) بَحْث	I a to do research (in)
بَحْث ج أَبْحاث\بُحوث	research
البَحْث والتَنْمِيّة	research and development
بحث ← بحوث	
بَراءة اِخْتِراع	patent
بِرْميل\بَرْميل ج بَراميل	barrel
بَضائع	goods
بَطّاريّة	battery
بِلاسْتيك	plastic (n.)
بِناء	construction (n.)
بِنائي	construction (adj.)

بيانات see علم

well (n.) f. بِئْر ج آبار

backlog تَأَخُّر

test, experiment تَجْرِبة ج تَجارِب

test, trial تَجْريب

experimental, see دراسة تَجْريبي

assembly, see خطّ تَجْميع

see اتّفاقية, حملة, مفاوضة تَحسين

V to specialise (in) تَخصّص (ل\ب\في)

planning تَخْطيط

backlog تَراكُم

design تَصْميم

see تصميمي تفكير

localisation تَعْريب

inspection تَفْتيش

design thinking تَفْكير تَصْميمي

technology تِقْنيّة

refining (n.), see محطّة تَكْرير

analog(ue) تَناظُري

see بحث تنمية

diversification تَنَوُّع

scaling-up تَوَسُّع

جدّد II to renovate, modernise

جَدْوَى feasibility

جرّب ب II to test, experiment with

جَرْد inventory

جمّع II to assemble (parts)

جملة see إنتاج

جِهاز ج أجْهِزة device, set

جِهاز حَفْر drilling rig

جودة see مراقبة

جِيولوجي geological, geologist

حدّث II to modernise

حَديد iron (n.)

حَرارة heat, see درجة

حركة see دراسة

حَفّار driller

حفر see جهاز

حَفَر حَفْر I i to drill

حَلّ ج حُلول solution

حَمْلة تَحْسين productivity drive/campaign
الإنْتاجيّة

خارج see نقل

خارِجي see مصدر, استعان

خارِطة طَريق road map

نفط ,زيت see خام

طاقة see خَضْراء

خَطّ تَجْميع assembly line

دائرة ج دَوَائر circuit

دِراسة تَجْريبيّة pilot study

دِراسة الوَقْت وَالحَرَكة time and motion study

دَرَجة degree

دَرَجة حَرارة temperature

دشّن II to launch

دائرة ← دوائر

دَوْرة cycle

رائد groundbreaking

رَقْمي digital

ركّب II to install

زُجاج glass (n.)

زَيْت ج زُيُوت oil

زَيْت خام crude oil

زيّت II to lubricate

زيت ← زيوت

سِعة capacity

,صحّة ,إجراءات see safety, سَلامة
مسؤول

و سم سلع see

سِماد ج أَسْمِدة fertiliser

شحّم II to lubricate

شَحَن (ب) شَحْن I a to load (with), charge (battery)

شَرِكة corporate

شغّل ه II to operate s.t.

لوحة شمسي see

صان صِيَانة I ū to maintain

الصِحّة والسَلامة health and safety

صلّح II to repair

صمّم II to design

صِناعة industry

صِناعي synthetic, artificial, see قطا ع

صَنَع صَنْع\صُنْع I a to manufacture

صنّف II to classify

صَهْريج ج صَهاريج tank (storage for gas or liquid)

صِيَانة maintenance, see صان

ضاعف III to maximise

ألياف see ضوئي

طاقة energy

طاقة خَضْراء green energy

طبّق ه على II to apply s.t to s.t.

طَرَح طَرْح I *a* to launch

خارطة see طَرِيق

حسب الطَّلَب custom-made

عاطِل idle (machinery)

عالِم ج عُلَماء scientist

عَصْري cutting-edge

عَقْليّة mindset

عِلْم البَيَانات data science

عالم ← علماء

عِلْمي scientific

عَمَليّة operation, process

عَيْب ج عُيُوب defect

غاز gas

قطعة see غِيار

فَنّي technical, technician

فولاذ steel (n.)

قاس قَيْس\قِيَاس I *i* to measure

قُدْرة capacity

قِطاع صِناعي industry

قِطْعة غِيَار spare part

قِطْعة ج قِطَع part, component

قلّل II to minimise

قَوِي robust

قيس see قاس

كرّر II to refine

كَسْر ج كُسور fraction (of crude oil)

كَمّيّة quantity, see مراقبة

كَهْرَباء electricity, see اختصاصي

كَهْرَبائي electric(al)

كيمياء chemistry

كيميائي chemical, chemist

لَوْحة شَمْسيّة solar panel

مادّة أوَّليّة raw material

مادّة ج مَوادّ material (n.)

مُتَطَوِّر cutting-edge

مُحَرِّك engine

مَحَطّة إنْتاج production station

مَحَطّة تَكْرير refinery

مُحَلِّل analyst

مُخْرَجات (pl.) output

مرفق ← مرافق

مُراقَبة الجُودة quality control

مُراقَبة كَمّيّة quantity control

مركز ← مراكز

مَرْفِق ج مَرافِق utility (electricity, gas etc.)

مَرْكَز نُفُوذ powerhouse

مَسْؤُول سَلامة safety officer

مشغل ← مشاغِل

مَشْغَل ج مَشاغِل workshop

مصنع ← مصانع

استعان see مصدر

مَصْدَر خارِجي outsource

مَصْنَع ج مَصانِع factory

مِضَخّة pump

معمل ← معامِل

وضع see معايير

اقتصاد see معرفة

مُعَطَّل idle (machinery)

مَعْمَل ج مَعامِل laboratory

مَعيب defective

مُفاوَضة تَحْسين productivity bargaining
الإِنْتاجيّة

وضع see مقارنة

مُقاوِل contractor

مُنْتَج product

مُنْتِج productive, producer

مُهَنْدِس engineer

مادة ← مواد

مُوَرِّد supplier

مُوَلِّد generator

ميكانيكي mechanic, mechanical

ميكانيكيّة mechanics

مِئَوِي celsius

نَفْط خام crude oil

مركز نفوذ see

نَقْص shortage

نَقَل إلى الخارج نَقْل I *u* to offshore

نُمُوّ growth

نَمُوذَج prototype

نَوْبة shift (period of work)

نوّع II to diversify

هَجين hybrid

هَنْدَسة engineering

وَسْم السِلَع branding

وَضْع مَعايِير المُقارَنة benchmarking

دراسة وقت see

وَقود fuel

7. PUBLICITY & MARKETING

اِتِّجاه	trend
وسائط see اجتماعي	
مبيع see ,(.gross (adj	إجْمالي
رسالة see إخباري	
براءة see اختراع	
اِسْتِطْلاع رأي	survey
استغلّ ه ه	X to exploit (fairly or unfairly)
اِسْتِغْلالي	profiteering
اِسْتِمارة طَلَب	order form
اِسْتيراد	import(ation)
مراقبة ,قائمة see ,سعر ← أسعار	
سوق ← أسواق	
اشترى	X to buy
شعار ← أشعرة	
صاحب ← أصحاب	
إعْلان	advertisement, advertising (n.),
وسائل ,مؤلّف ,لوحة see	
إعْلان جَماعي بِالبَريد	mail shot
أعلن	IV to advertise
أغرق	IV to dump (sell at low price)

متجر أقسام see

تسويق إلكتروني see

آلة بَيْع vending machine

اِمْتِيَاز concession, franchise,

صاحب see

انترنت ندوة see

اِنْتِقائي selective

هدف ← أهداف

باع بَيْع\مَبيع ī I to sell

بائع ج باعة\sound salesman

بَراءة اِخْتِراع patent

بريد إعلان , طلب see

بريدي طلب see

بَيَان صُحُفي press release

نقطة ,باع ,آلة see sale, بَيْع ج بُيُوع

لِلْبَيْع for/on sale

لِلْبَيْع أوْ لِلرَدّ on sale or return

بيع ← بيوع

تاجر (ه ب\في) III to trade (with s.o. in s.t.)

تَبادُل exchange

محلّ تجارة see

تجاري see تسويق, تمييز, حاجز, سجلّ,
سمعة, شهرة, علامة, قيمة,
ملحق, ولاء

بِالتَجْزِئَة retail (adj./adv.)

تَرْخيص licensing

تَرْويج promotion, merchandising

تَسْعير pricing

تَسَلْسُل التَوْزيع distribution chain

تسويق see حملة, شركة, قناة

تَسْويق إلِكْتَرَوْني e-marketing

تَسْويق تِجاري commercialisation

تَسْويق عبر الهَاتِف telemarketing

تَشَبُّع السوق market saturation

تَصْفية clearance (sale)

تَصْميم الجْرافيك graphic design

تَعْبِئة وَتَغْليف packaging

تَعْريب localisation

تَفْضيلي preferential

تَقَدُّم traction

تقسيط see شراء

تَكْليف ج تَكاليف cost

تلفز IQ to televise   no vb. n.

تَمْييز تِجاري branding

تَنافُسي competitive

وسائط تواصل see وسائط تواصل

تسلسل توزيع see توزيع

ثِقة المُسْتَهْلِك consumer confidence

جارٍ going, current (rate, price etc.)

تصميم جرافيك see تصميم

إعلان جماعي see إعلان

جُمْلة wholesale (n.)

بالجُمْلة wholesale (adj./adv.)

حاجِز تِجاري trade barrier

حَدّي marginal

سوق حرّ see سوق

حُزْمة ج حُزَم bundle

حَصْري exclusive

حِصّة ج حِصَص quota

حِصّة في السوق market share

حَمْلة ج حَمَلات campaign, drive

حَمْلة تَسْويق marketing campaign

خِدْمة العُمَلاء customer service

خَصْم discount

خفّض ه II to reduce s.t.

دِراسة سوق market research/study

دِعايَة publicity, advertising

ديموغْرافيا demographics

استطلاع رأي see استطلاع

رِبْحيّة profitability

رَخيص cheap, inexpensive

بيع ردّ see ردّ

رِسالة إخْباريّة newsletter

متحدّث رسمي see رسمي

رُسوم مَعْلوماتيّة infographics

رِضا العَميل customer satisfaction

رِعايَة sponsorship

رَقْم المَبيعات sales turnover

روّج II to promote

زائد excess, surplus (adj.)

زَبون ج زَبائن customer

زَخْم traction

ساوم ه\ب في\على III to bargain with s.o. over s.t.

سائد going, current (adj.)

سِجِلّ الطلَبات التِجاريّة order book

سعّر II to price

سِعْر ج أسْعار price

سِعْر الطلَب asking price

سِعْر مَعْروض offer price

سلعة ← goods سِلَع pl.

سِلَع كَماليّة luxury goods

سِلَع مُعَمّرة durable products

سِلْعة ج سِلَع commodity

سُمْعة تِجاريّة goodwill

سوداء see سوق

سوق ج أسْوَاق market, marketplace, see تشبع, f.
قوّى, دراسة, حرّ, حصّة

سوّق II to market

سوق حُرّة free market

سوق سَوْداء black market

سوق مُتَخَصِّصة niche market

سوق ناشئة emerging market

شَبَكة network

شِراء purchasing

شِراء بِالتَقْسيط hire-purchase,

purchase by installment

شرائي see قوة

شَرِكة تَسْويق marketing company

شِعار ج أشْعِرة logo, slogan sound\

goodwill شُهْرة (تِجاريّة)

concessionaire, franchise holder صاحِب اِمْتِياز

exports صادِرات

see بيان صحفي

fact sheet صَحيفة وَقائع

II to export صدَّر

I u to demand, order (goods) طلَب من ه طلَب

demand, order (of goods), see طلَب

عرض ,سعر ,سجلّ ,استمارة

نموذج

mail order طلَب بَريدي\بالبَريد

on demand/request عند الطلَب

I i to exhibit, offer عَرَض على ه عَرْض

offer (n.) عَرْض ج عُروض

supply and demand العَرْض وَالطلَب

عرض ⟵ عروض

customer relationship عَلاقات العُمَلاء

see خدمة عملاء

trade mark, see قيمة, ولاء عَلامَة تِجاريّة

see رضا عميل

expensive غالٍ

seasonal فَصْلي

قابِل لِلقِياس	measurable
قائمة أسْعار	price list
قَسيمة	coupon
قِطاع	segment
فَناة تَسْويق	marketing channel
قُوَّة شِرائيّة	purchase/purchasing power
قُوَى السوق	market forces
قابل see قياس	
قيمة العَلامة التِجاريّة	brand equity
كاتالوج	catalog(ue)
كُتَيِّب	brochure
كلّف (ه) ه II	to cost (s.o.) s.t.
گمالي luxury (adj.), see سلع	
كوبون	coupon
لَوْحة إعْلانات	billboard, noticeboard
مَبيع sale, see باع, رقم	
مَبيعات اِجْماليّة pl.	gross sales, sales turnover
مَتْجَر ج مَتاجِر	shop, store
مَتْجَر (ذو) أقْسام	department store
مُتَحَدِّث رَسْمي	spokesperson
سوق see متخصّص	
مُتَداوَل	(in) circulation

مَتْن durable

مَحَلّ تِجارة trade outlet

مُخَفَّض reduced

مُراقَبة أسْعار price control

مُرْتَفِع high, rising, raised

مَزاد auction

مُسْتَعْمَل second-hand

مُسْتَهْلِك consumer, see ثقة

مُشْتَرٍ buyer

مُشْتَرًى purchase (thing purchased)

مُشْتَرَيَات purchasing (n.) pl.

مَعْرِض ج مَعارِض exhibition

معروض see سعر

مَعْرُوضات exhibit(s) pl.

معلوماتي see رسوم

معمّر see سلع

مُلْحَق تِجاري commercial attaché

مُمَثِّل representative

مُنافَسة competition

مُنْخَفِض low

مَنْزِلي door-to-door (adj.)

مُواصَفات specifications

عند المُوافَقة on approval

مُوَرِّد supplier

مَوْسِمي seasonal

مُؤَلِّف إعْلانات (advertising) copywriter

سوق see ناشئة

نَدْوَة على الانْتِرْنِت webinar

نُقْطة البَيْع point of sale

نُمُوّ growth

نَموذَج طلَب order form

تسويق see هاتف

هَدَف ج أهْداف target

وزّع II to distribute

وَسائل إعْلان advertising media

وَسائط التَواصُل الإجْتِماعي social media

وَسيط intermediary

صحيفة see وقائع

وَكيل ج وُكَلاء agent

وَلاء لِلعَلامة التِجاريّة brand loyalty

8. STORAGE, TRANSPORT & TRAVEL

أَبْحَر IV to set sail

برج ← أبراج

إجْراءات formalities (customs etc.)

أُجْرة fare, freight charge

حجم ← أحجام

إذْن permit (n.)

إرْسال despatch

رصيف ← أرصفة

أسطول ← أساطيل

استأجر X to charter

خدمات see استقبال

استورد X to import

أُسْطول ج أساطيل fleet (ships, aircraft, vehicles)

سفر ← أسفار

إشارة signal

مخزن, بضائع see إشراف

إشْغال occupancy

صنف ← أصناف

طنّ ← أطنان

إعْلان declaration (customs etc.)

درجة أعمال see

إقامة accommodation

أقلع IV to take off (of aircraft)

تذكرة إلكتروني see

متر ← أمتار

أمْتِعة baggage

إمْدادات logistics pl.

قائمة ,قاعة انتظار see

اِنْتِقال relocation, transition

أودع ه ه IV to consign/entrust to s.o. s.t.

درجة أولى see (f. adj.)

تذكرة إياب see

مخزن إيداع see

باخِرة ج بَوَاخِر steamer

ناقلة بترول see

بحري sea (adj.), see رحلة

بُرْج التَحَكُّم control tower

بَرّي land (adj.), see نقل ,بوليصة

بِضاعة ج بَضائع goods (s. also used as pl.)

بِضاعة مَحْظورة prohibited goods

بِضاعة\بَضائع مُودَعة bonded goods
بِإشْراف الجُمْرُك

بِطاقة صُعود boarding pass

بَعَث (ه) ه\ب بَعْث I a to send s.t. (to s.o.)

بَوّابة gate

باخرة ⟵ بواخر

بوليصة شَحْن bill of lading

بوليصة شَحْن بَرّي waybill

بوليصة شَحْن جَوِّي air waybill

بَيَان declaration (customs etc.),

صحيفة see

بَيَان حُمولة manifest

بيئي see سياحة

تأْخير see غرامة

تأْشيرة visa

تحكّم see برج

تَخْزين storage

تَخْليص clearance

تَذْكَرة ج تَذاكِر ticket

تَذْكَرة إلِكْتْرونيّة e-ticket

تَذْكَرة ذَهاب وَإِياب return ticket

تَسْجيل خُروج check-out

تَسْجيل دُخول check-in

تَفْتيش inspection

شحن see تفريغ

تَكْديس stacking

سريع see تلف

تَوجّه إلى V to head for

تَوَقُّف layover, stopover

تَوْقيت غْرينِتْش Greenwich Mean Time, GMT

جَرَد ه جَرْد I u to make an inventory of, take

stock of

مخزن, بضائع see جُمْرُك ج جَمارِك customs, see

مخلّص, رسوم see جمركي

بِالجُمْلة bulk (adj.), in bulk (adv.)

جَواز سَفَر passport

خطوط, بوليصة see جَوّي air (adj.), see,

وثيقة

زائد see حاجة

حاوِية container

حَجَز حَجْز I u/i to reserve

حَجْم ج أحْجام\حُجوم volume, bulk (n.)

سكّة see حديدي

ميناء, منطقة, سوق see حرّ

حَقيبة ج حَقائب suitcase, travelling case

(pl. = luggage)

حَمَّال porter

حَمَل حَمْل I *i* to carry, convey

حُمولة cargo, freight, see بيان

حَوْض السُفُن dock

خِدْمات (.pl) الاسْتِقْبال reception service

خُروج exit (action), see تسجيل

خزّن II to store, stock

خَطّ سَيْر route

خطر see موادّ

خُطوط جَوِّيّة airline(s)

دُخول entry (action), see تسجيل

دَرَجة أُولى first class

دَرَجة رِجال الأَعْمال business class

دَرَجة سياحيّة economy class

ذهاب see تذكرة

راحة see وسائل

رافِعة crane

راكِب ج رُكّاب passenger

رُبّان ج رُبابِنة\رَبابين (ship's) captain

رتّب (في مَخْزَن) II to stow

رجال see درجة

رِحْلة trip, journey, excursion, flight,
see مخطّط

رِحْلة بَحْريّة cruise

رِحْلة عَمَل business trip

رِحْلة مُباشِرة direct flight

رَسْم ج رُسوم duty, tax, fee

رسى see رسو

رسم see رسوم

رُسوم جُمْرُكيّة custom duties

رَسَى intr. رَسْو I *i* to berth, dock

رَصيف ج أرْصِفة wharf, quay, pier, platform

راكب → ركّاب

رَكِب ه رُكوب I *a* to get on/in (transport)

زار زِيَارة I *ū* to visit

زائد excess(ive), surplus (adj.)

زائد عن الحاجة surplus to requirements

زائر ج زُوّار visitor

زار see زيارة

سافر III to travel

ساق سِيَاقة I *ū* to drive

سائح tourist

سائق driver

سَريع التَلَف perishable

جواز see, journey سَفَر ج أسْفار

حوض see سفن

مطبخ, حوض see, ship سَفينة ج سُفُن

سِكّة حَديديّة railway

(في\من) السوق الحُرّة duty-free

درجة see سياحي

سِيَاحة tourism

سِيَاحة بيئيّة ecotourism

سِيَاحة عَلاجيّة medical tourism

ساق see سياقة

خطّ see سير

"سيف" *transcription of* c.i.f. (cost,

insurance and freight),

شاحِنة truck, lorry, van

شَحْن load, cargo, freight, shipment,

وثيقة , بوليصة see

شَحَن (ه) ب شَحْن I *a* to load (a carrier) with s.t.

شَحَن ه شَحْن I *a* to load (goods)

شَحْنة ج شَحَنات lading, consignment, freight

شَحْن وَتَفْريغ stevedoring

شحنة ← شحنات

شَهادة مَنْشأ certificate of origin

صادِرات exports

صَحيفة بَيَانات data sheet

صدّر (إلى) II to export (to)

صَعِد (إلى) صُعود I a to embark (on)

صِنْف ج أصْناف grade

صعد ,بطاقة see صعود

ناقلة see ضخمة

طار طَيَران I ī to fly

طاقِم مَقْصورة cabin crew

طائرة aircraft, see مطبخ

طَريق ج طُرُق road m./f.

عن طَريق via, by way of

طُنّ ج أطْنان ton(ne)

طَيَّار (aircraft) pilot

مضيف ,طار see طَيَران flight,

عجّل II to expedite

عَرَبة carriage (vehicle)

مصروفات see عرضي

سياحة see علاجي

رحلة see عمل

غادر ه III to leave, depart from

غَرامة تَأْخير demurrage

توقيت see غرينيتش

فتّش II to inspect

فرّغ ه II to unload (a cargo)

"فوب" *transcription of* f.o.b. (free on

board)

قاد قِيادة I *ū* to drive

قاعة اِنْتِظار waiting room

قائمة اِنْتِظار waiting list

قِطار ج قُطُر \ sound train (n.)

قطَر قطْر I *u* to tow

قاد see قيادة

كدَس ه كدْس I *i* to stack

كدّس ه II to stack

لافِتة placard

لوجِسْتِيَات .pl logistics

رحلة see مباشر

مِتْر ج أمْتار meter/metre

مِتْر مُربَّع square meter/metre

مِتْر مُكعَّب cubic meter/metre

على مَتْن on board (also in cst.)

مُتَوَفِّر in stock

مُحْتَوَيَات contents

مَحَطّة station, terminal

مَحْظُور see بضاعة

مَحْفُوظ see بضاعة

مَخْزَن ج مَخازِن store(room), warehouse, see رتّب

مَخْزَن إيداع بِإشْراف الجُمْرُك bonded warehouse

مَخْزُون stock (n.)

مُخَطَّط رِحْلة itinerary

مُخَلِّص جُمْرُكي custom broker

مَدْفُوع النَقْل carriage paid

مرسًى → مراسٍ

مركب → مراكب

متر see مربّع

مُرْسَل consigned, deposited

مُرْسِل consignor, depositor

مُرْسَل إليه consignee. depository

مَرْسًى ج مَراسٍ anchorage, berth, mooring

مُرْشِد (ship's) pilot

مَرْكَب ج مَراكِب vessel (boat, ship)

مُرُور transit

مُسَبَّق advance (adj.)

مُسْتَوْدَع	depot, warehouse
مُسْتَوْدَع وَقود	fuel bunker
مُسْتَوْرَدات	imports
مَصْروفات عَرَضيّة	incidentals
مُضيف طَيَران	flight attendant
مَطار	airport
مَطْبَخ (سَفينة\طائرة)	galley
مُغادَرة	departure
مُفَتِّش	inspector
مُقاصّة	set-off
مَقْصورة	compartment, طاقم see
مَقْطورة	trailer
مَكان وُصول	destination
مكعّب	متر see
مِلاحة	shipping, navigation
مُنْحَدَر	ramp
منشأ	شهادة see
مِنْطَقة حُرّة	free zone
مَوادّ خَطِرة pl.	hazardous material
ميناء ← مَوَانٍ\موانئ	
مودع	بضائع see
ميناء ج مَوَانٍ\مَوانئ m./f.	port

ميناء حُرّة(ة) free port

ناقِل carrier (ship, vehicle)

ناقِلة بِتْرُول oil tanker (ship)

ناقِلة ضَخْمة supertanker

نَزَل نُزول I *i* to land (of an aircraft)

نُزول landing, stopover

نَفَق ج أنْفاق tunnel

نَقْل transport, see مدفوع

نَقْل بَرّي road haulage

هِجْرة immigration

وَارِدات imports

وَثيقة شَحْن جَوّي air waybill

وَسائل الراحة amenities

وَصَل (إلى) وُصول I *i* to arrive (at)

وُصول arrival, see مكان

وَقود fuel

9. PERSONNEL

أبدال ← بدل

إبْقاء retention

أَبَوِي paternalist(ic)

أبوّة see إجازة

إجازات see رصيد

إجازة leave, see رصيد

إجازة أُبُوَّة paternity leave

إجازة أُمومة maternity leave

إجازة سَنَوِيّة annual leave

إجازة مُتَراكِمة accrued leave

إجازة مَرَضيّة sick leave

اجتماعي see ضمان

أجْر ج أُجور wage, see حدّ

إجْراءات تَظَلُّم grievance procedure

أُجور ← أجر

أحْكام وَشُروط terms and conditions

اختبار see فترة

إدارة شُؤون المُوَظَّفِين personnel administration/

management

أدنى see حدّ

راتب see أساسي

استحقّ X to merit

علاوة see استحقاق

استخدم X to recruit

استقال (عن\من) X to resign (from)

اِسْتِنْزاف attrition

إشْعار notice, notification

صاحب ← أصحاب

فائدة , شغل see إضافي

أضرب IV to strike

إعادة تَوْظيف reinstatement

أقْدَميّة seniority

أمْن وَظيفي job security

إجازة see أمومة

اِنْتِداب secondment

إنْذار warning

إنْهاء غَيْر مَشْروع wrongful termination

أوقف (عن) IV to suspend (from)

موظّف see بديل

بَدَل ج أبْدال\sound allowance

بَرْنامَج عَمَل مَرِن flexible working

رأس see بشري

بَطالة unemployment

تَأْديبي disciplinary

تَحْكيم arbitration

تَدْريب training

تَدْريب أثناء العَمَل on-the-job training

تَسْريح dismissal, lay-off

تَسْليم handover

تَضارُب مَصالِح conflict of interests

تظلّم see إجراءات

تَعْويض compensation

تَغَيُّب absenteeism

تقاعد VI to retire

تَقاعُد retirement, see معاش

تَقْليص retrenchment

تَقْييم المُوَظَّفين staff appraisal

تَقْييم الوَظيفة job evaluation

تَكاليف المَعيشة cost of living

تَمْييز (ضدّ) discrimination (against)

تَناسِبي pro-rated

تَنْفيذي executive (adj.), see مُوظَّف

تَوْصيف وَظيفة job description

تَوْصِية recommendation

تَوْظيف recruitment, staffing,

و كالة , إعادة see

جَدْوَل رَوَاتِب pay scale, payroll

دوام جزئي see

مساومة جماعي see

زيادة , زائد حاجة see

حادِث ج حَوَادِث accident

حَجْم العَمَل workload

حَدّ أدْنى لِلأَجْر minimum wage

حَرَكيّة mobility (workforce, jobs etc.)

حِساب مَصْروفات expense account

حَكَم ج حُكّام referee

بِحُكْم الوَظيفة ex-officio

حادث ← حوادث

خارِجي external

خالف III to violate

وظائف خالي see

خِبْرة experience

نهاية , شروط خِدْمة service, see

خفّض II to downsize

خَفْض دَرَجة demotion

خَفْض الراتِب salary cut

داخِلي internal

دافِع ج دَوَافِع motive

درجة grade, see خفض

دافع ← دوافع

دَوَافِع العَمَل motivation

دَوَام جُزْئي part-time

دَوَام كامِل full-time

رابط III to picket intr.

راتِب أساسي base salary

راتِب ج رَوَاتِب salary, see خفض، سلفة

راتِب صافٍ net(t) salary, take-home pay

راتِب مُتَأخِّر back pay

رأْس مال بَشَري human capital

راقب III to supervise

رُتْبة ج رُتَب grade

رُخْصة عَمَل work permit

رَشْوة ج رَشَاوى bribe

رَصيد الإجازات leave balance

رَفاهيّة welfare

رقّى II to promote

رَمْزي token (adj., payment, strike etc.)

رواتب ← راتب, see جدول, خفض,
سلّم

رَوَاتِب مُتَساوِيّة equal pay

زائد عن حاجة redundant

زَميل ج زُمَلاء colleague

زِيَادة عن حاجة redundancy

سِجِلّ record (n.)

ساوم (ه على\في) III to bargain (with s.o. over s.t.)

سُلْفة (على الراتِب) salary advance

سُلَّم رَوَاتِب salary range

سلوك see سوء

سنوي see إجازة, معاش

سُوء سُلوك misconduct

شاغر see منصب

شخصي see شهادة

شَرْط ج شُروط (pre-)condition

شروط see أحكام

شُروط الخِدْمة terms of service

شُغْل إضافي overtime (work)

شَكْوَى ج شَكاوَى complaint

شَهادة شَخْصيّة (candidate's) reference

شؤون see إدارة, مدير

employer صاحِب العَمَل

see صافٍ راتب

see صغير موظّف

see صناعي علاقات

social security ضَمان اِجْتِماعي

see طبّي فحص

application, request, see نموذج طلَب

working conditions ظُروف العَمَل

unemployed عاطِل (عن العَمَل)

workman عامِل ج عُمّال

see عاملة قوة

I i to dismiss (from) عَزَل (عن) عَزْل

penalty عُقُوبة

industrial relations عَلاقات صِناعيّة

increment, pay raise/rise عِلاوَة

merit raise/rise عِلاوَة اِسْتِحْقاق

see ,عامل ,مندوب ,نقابة عمّال ←

see ,برنامج ,تدريب ,حجم عمل
,دوافع ,رخصة ,صاحب
ظروف, عاطل, وزارة, وزير

racism عُنْصُرِيّة

in lieu of عِوَضًا عن

عيّن ه (...اً)	II to appoint (as ...)
فائدة إضافيّة	fringe benefit
فَتْرة اِخْتِبار	probation period
فَحْص طِبّي	medical examination
فَحْص نَفْسي	psychological examination/test
قُوَّة عامِلة	manpower
كاتِب ج كُتّاب	clerk
دوام see كامل	
موظّف see كبير	
كاتب ← كتّاب	
موظّف see كتابي	
كَفاءة	qualification
رأس see مال	
ماهِر	skilled
مدير see مباشر	
راتب see متأخر	
إجازة see متراكم	
رواتب see متساوي	
مُتَقاعِد	pensioner
مَحْسوبيّة	nepotism
مُدير ج مُدَراء\sound	manager, director
مُدير شُؤون المُوظَّفين	personnel manager

مُدير مُباشِر line manager

مُراقِب supervisor, foreman

مُرَشَّح candidate

إجازة مرضي see إجازة مرضي

برنامج مَرِن flexible, see برنامج

مَزايَا benefits

مُساوَمة جَماعيّة collective bargaining

مُسْتَخْدِم employer

مشغل ← مشاغل

مُشْرِف supervisor

إنهاء مشروع see إنهاء

مَشْغَل مُقْفَل closed shop (workplace where all employees must belong to one specified trade union)

تضارب مصالح see تضارب

مُصالَحة conciliation

حساب مصروفات see حساب

وظائف مطلوب see وظائف

مَعاش (تَقاعُد) (retirement) pension

مَعاش سَنَوِي annuity

تكاليف معيشة see تكاليف

مُغْتَرِب expatriate

مُقابَلة interview

مشغل see مقفل

مُكَافأة remuneration, bonus, gratuity

مُمَثِّل نِقابة shop steward, trade union
representative

مُنازَعة dispute

منصب ← مناصب

مُناوَبة shift (period of work)

مَنْدوب (العُمّال) shop steward, trade union
representative

مَنْصِب شاغِر vacancy

مِهْنة ج مِهَن career, profession

مُوَظَّف employee, see إدارة ,تقييم ,مدير

مُوَظَّف بَديل replacement employee

مُوَظَّف تَنْفيذي executive (n.)

مُوَظَّف صَغير junior staff employee

مُوَظَّف كَبير senior staff employee

مُوَظَّف كِتابي clerk

مُؤَهَّل qualified, skilled

مُؤَهَّل (ل) elegible (for)

مُؤَهِّل qualification (for a job)

فحص see نَفْسي

ممثل see نقابة

نِقابة عُمّال trade union

نَقَل نَقْل I u to transfer

نَموذَج طَلَب application form

نِهاَية الخِدْمة end-of-service

نِيَابة deputyship

نِيَابةً عن acting/deputising for

وِزارة العَمَل Ministry of Labor/Labour

وَزير العَمَل Minister of Labor/Labour

وظيفة → وظائف

وَظائف خاليّة situations vacant

وَظائف مَطْلوبة situations wanted

وظّف II to recruit

وَظيفة ج وَظائف job, post, see تقييم, توصيف,
حكم, وصف

وظيفي see أمن

وَكالة تَوْظيف employment agency/bureau

10. MEETINGS & CONFERENCES

اِتَّخذ	VIII to adopt
اِجْتِماع meeting, see محضر	
اِجْتِماع اِفْتِراضي	virtual meeting
اِجْتِماع غَيْر عادي	extraordinary meeting
اِجْتِماع مَجْلِس إدارة	board meeting
اِجْتِماع هاتِفي	conference call
اِجْتِماع هَجين	hybrid meeting
اجتمع	VIII to have a meeting
إجْماع	consensus
بالإجْماع، إجْماعي	unanimous
أجْمع (على)	IV to be unanimous (on)
احتجّ (على)	VIII to protest (against)
حدث ← أحداث	
اختصر	VIII to summarise
أخرى see أيّة	
خطاب ← أخطبة	
إدارة see اجتماع	
آراء ← رأي, تبادل see	
أرجأ	IV to adjourn, suspend
إرْشادات	guidelines

إرشادي see تعليمات

استأنف ه X to resume

استنتج (من) X to deduce/infer (from)

اسم see متحدّث

أسماء see تفقّد

أُطُر مَرْجِعيّة terms of reference

اِعْتِذار apology

اعتذر عن الغِياب VIII to apologise for absence

اعترض (على) VIII to object (to)

عضو ← أعضاء

أعطى ه الكَلِمة IV to give the floor to

إعْلان announcement, communiqué

مركز ,جدول ,أيّة see أعمال

اِفْتِتاحي inaugural

واقع ,اجتماع see افتراضي

اِقْتِراع بِالشُكْر vote of thanks

اِقْتِراع سِرّي secret ballot

اقترح VIII to move, propose

اقترع (على) VIII to ballot (on)

ألقى IV to deliver (a speech etc.)

مؤتمر see إلكتروني

مكان ← أماكن

VIII to abstain (from) امتنع (عن)

مكان ← أمكنة

VIII to co-opt, elect انتخب

see مؤتمر إنترنت

VIII to find fault with انتقد هـ\على

IV to summarise أوجز

II to support, second, endorse أيّد

any other business أيّة أَعْمال أُخْرى

III to exaggerate, overstate بالغ في

web cast بَثّ شَبَكي

live stream بَثّ مُباشِر

I a to discuss بَحَث هـ بَحْث ج بُحوث

see نطاق , عرض بحث

program(me) بَرْنامَج ج بَرامِج

see سمعي بصري

mission, delegation بَعْثة

on the basis of بِناءً على

constructive (idea etc.) بَنّاء

item بَنْد ج بُنود

press release بَيَان صُحُفي

exchange of views تَبادُل الآراء

V to adopt (a resolution etc.) تبنّى

تذكّر V to remember, bear in mind

تراجم see ترجم

ترأّس V to preside

ترجم تَرْجَمة ج تَراجِم IQ to translate

ترجم شَفَهيًّا IQ to interpret

ترجمة see ترجم

تَرْجَمة مُتَزامَنة simultaneous translation

تَسْجيل registration

تشاور VI to confer

تَصْويت على\بِالثِقة vote of confidence

تَعْديل amendment

تَعْليمات إرْشاديّة guidelines

تعليمي see دورة

تَغْذية راجِعة feedback

تَفَقُّد الأَسْماء roll call

توتّر see كسر

تَوْجيهي guiding (principle etc.)

ثانيةً see دعا

ثقة see تصويت

جَدْوَل أعْمال agenda

جَلْسات مُتَوازيّة parallel sessions

جَلْسة session, sitting

جَلْسة خاصّة special session

جَلْسة عامّة plenary session

مكان see جلوس

جَمْعيّة عُمومِيّة general assembly

حاسِم conclusive

حَدَث ج أَحْداث event

حُزْمة مُؤْتَمر conference pack

attendance, see عدم حُضور

حَلَقة دِراسِيّة شَبَكيّة webinar

جلسة see خاصّ

خِطاب ج أَخْطِبة speech, address

خُطْبة ج خُطَب speech, address

حلقة see دراسي

III to circulate داول ه

لجنة see دائم

حلقة see دراسي

دَعا ه ه دَعْوة I ū to convene

دَعا ه ه ثانيةً I ū to reconvene

ردّ, دعا see دعوة

دَوْرة تَعْليمِيّة tutorial (n.)

دَوّن II to note

ذَكَر ذِكْر I u to mention

ذكّر ه ه   II to remind s.o. of s.t.

ذهني   see عصف

راجع   see تغذية

راجع ه   III to review, reiterate, revert to

رَأَس ه رِئاسة\رِياسة   I *a* to preside over, chair

رَأْي ج آراء   opinion

رَدّ على الدَعْوَة   RSVP

رحّب ب   II to welcome

رِئاسة\رِياسة   see رأس

رَئيس ج رُؤَساء   chairman

رَئيسي   keynote (adj.)

زِيارة مَوْقِع   site visit

ساند   III to support

سبب   see نقد

سجّل   II to place on record

سرّي   see اقتراع

سلّم ب   II to concede

سَمْعي بَصَري   audiovisual

شبكي   see حلقة ,بثّ

شفهيًّا   see ترجم

شكر   see اقتراع

صالح   see صوّت

صالة hall

صحفي see بيان

صدّق على II to approve

صرّح II to declare

صوّت (على\لِصالِح\ضدّ) II to vote (on/for/against)

ضِمْني tacit

طاوِلة مُسْتَديرة round table

طلَب فُرْصة الكَلام طلَب I u to ask for the floor

عادي see اجتماع

عامّ see جلسة

عَدَم حُضور no-show

عَرْض ج عُروض presentation

عَرَض لِلبَحْث عَرْض I i to table

عرض ← عروض

عَصْف ذِهْني brainstorming

عُضْو ج أعْضاء member

عَقَد عَقْد I u to hold (a conference etc.)

عمل see ورشة

عمومي see جمعيّة

عُنْوان ج عَناوين heading, title

غاب (عن) غِياب I i to be absent (from)

غائب absentee

غاب ,اعتذر see غياب

اجتماع see غير عادي

طلب see فرصة

لجنة see فرعي

قاطع III to interrupt

قاعة auditorium

قَرار resolution

كَسْر التَوَتُّر ice breaker

طلب see كلام

أعطى see كلمة

الكَلِمة مع ... ... has the floor

لامُؤْتَمَر unconference

لَجْنة دائِمة standing committee

لَجْنة فَرْعِيّة sub-committee

لَجْنة مُخَصَّصة ad-hoc committee

ناطق see لسان

بثّ see مباشر

مُبَكِّر early bird

مُتَحَدِّث speaker (person speaking)

مُتَحَدِّث بِاسْم spokesperson for (in cst.)

ترجمة see متزامن

جلسات see متوازي

مجلس see اجتماع

مُحادَثات talks

مُحاضَرة talk, lecture, address

مَحْضَر الإجْتِماع minutes

لجنة see مخصّص

مُخَطَّط layout

مُراقِب observer

أطر see مرجعي

مَرْكَز أعْمال business center/centre

طاولة see مستدير

مُشارِك participant

مُطلَق absolute (majority etc.)

مُقْتَرَح proposal

مُقَدِّمة premise

مَكان ج أمْكِنة\أماكِن venue

مَكان الجُلوس seating

مُلَخَّص summary, abstract

مُلْصَق poster

مُنْتَدَّى forum

مَنْدوب delegate

مُنَسِّق facilitator

مُنَظِّم organiser

مُؤْتَمَر	conference, convention, see حزمة
مُؤْتَمَر إِلِكْتْروني	e-conference
مُؤْتَمَر على الإِنْتِرِنت	web conference
مُؤَجَّل	deferred
زيارة see موقع	
ناطِق بِلِسان	spokesperson
نائِب ج نُوّاب	representative, delegate
نَدْوة	symposium
نِصاب	quorum
نظامي see نقطة	
نظر see وجهة	
نَفى نَفْي i I	to deny, repudiate
نَقَد نَقْد u I	to criticise
نُقْطة نِظاميّة	point of order
نائِب ← نوّاب	
هاتفي see اجتماع	
هجين see اجتماع	
واحِدًا واحِدًا	one-on-one
واقِع اِفْتِراضي	virtual reality
وَثيقة ج وَثائِق	document
وُجْهة نَظَر	point of view
وَرْشة عَمَل	workshop

وصّى ه ب II to recommend

وَفْد ج وُفُود delegation

وَفْقًا ل in accordance with

وفد ← وفود

وَقائع proceedings

ENGLISH INDEX

This index enables you *inter alia* to use the book also as an English-Arabic vocabulary. The numbers refer to pages. A superscript number ^{2} (etc.) after a page number indicates more than one entry of the English word on that page.

The sign ~ repeats the headword (or that part of it preceding the hyphen). The sign ≈ repeats the headword (or that part of it preceding the hyphen) but with an initial capital letter.

Having found an English word, you are advised to examine every entry of it, since its Arabic equivalent may vary with the context.

CPSIA information can be obtained
at www.ICGtesting.com
Printed in the USA
BVHW081343150721
611403BV00002B/5

9 781647 121617